S0-BNS-928

100s OF
FREE
THINGS
FOR TEACHERS

DAWN HARDY

Publications International, Ltd.

Dawn Hardy is a freelance writer and the author of *Absolutely Free!* and *Bargains by Mail for Baby and You.* She is a former contributing editor for *Freebies Magazine* and has written product reviews for *Parenting Magazine.*

ISBN: 0-7853-1511-X

CONTENTS

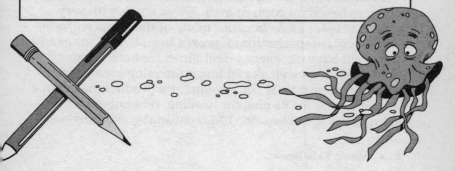

About This Book

Welcome to *Hundreds of Free Things for Teachers!* We hope this will prove to be an inspiring, useful source of classroom aids that serves you well in that never-ending quest to make teaching easier and more effective.

Extensive research into a wide range of national educational organizations, museums, cultural institutions, planetariums, science groups, and countless others has produced this wealth of materials that can be related to any course subject or grade level. Most of the items listed are absolutely free to qualified educators, and none cost more than a nominal $5. (Where fees are charged it's to help with the costs of production and postage so that these valuable tools can continue to be offered.)

This book is a listing of specific items, rather than a directory of catalogs. Our intention was to do the research for you, sifting through listings and sourcebooks to select free and low-cost items you can really use. Many of the items listed will introduce you to a source of numerous other classroom materials you'll want to explore. We have included some catalogs; these are generally resources so rich in potential that they deserved to be included or slightly unusual, perhaps unconventional, sources you might not be aware of.

Hundreds of Free Things for Teachers is divided into chapters based on content area. We've stuck with very general subject areas because many of the items we've selected defy categorization. A poster from NASA, for example, might have excellent possibilities for both science and math classes, as well as yielding interesting creative writing assignments. So if you encounter a product that's not a perfect match for its chapter heading, remember that some of the items just don't fit comfortably into any one category. Sourcebooks that can cover all or many subject areas have been included in the "Great Resources" chapter, along with materials that are just for teachers.

Every possible effort has been made to insure the up-to-the-minute accuracy of the information presented here. Each entry was verified at the time of publication as to its availability through the school year of 1995–96. However, there is no way to control possible changes after publication. Programs may lose funding, change address or phone number, etc. Companies may change their prices without warning, even if they have assured us that prices would remain the same through the 1995–96 school year. We've done our best to ensure that you'll have no unhappy surprises, but be aware that some items you request may no longer be available, or they may be offered at a different cost.

We hope you will use this book not only to help you locate individual items but also to tap into resources you might not have known about before. The lasting value is in the networking, the contact with far-flung colleagues in the same field, and the long-term resource development. Enjoy your research!

How to Request Your Free Things

To get the most out of this book with the least difficulty and ensure that you always receive what you requested, here are a few simple tips to keep in mind when making inquiries.

Each entry in this directory is precise, designed to tell you what you need to know about the organization and materials before you make your request, to prevent wasting anyone's valuable time and money. Be sure to follow all the instructions carefully, since variations can apply to each offer.

For many items, you can simply pick up the phone and request your information or materials. For others:

- It's always a good idea to write your requests on official school stationery. This identifies you as a professional educator and often means you'll receive more materials. Specify your grade, the subject you teach, and areas of interest; this will help the organization's staff serve you better and perhaps include additional items they have available that apply to your situation. Where official stationery is required to receive an item, we have specified that in the write-up, but again, it's always a good idea to use it anyway.

- Be sure to make your request using the exact title of the publication or item in question. This is especially important for materials from government agencies and larger organizations with huge volumes of mail.

- When an entry requires you to send a self-addressed stamped envelope, send a #10 business-size, long envelope with your name and address clearly printed on the front and with adequate first-class postage attached.

- If a write-up specifies that you must send a $9'' \times 12''$ self-addressed stamped envelope, remember that the higher $.54 first-class postage must be attached, not just a 32-cent stamp.

Perhaps most importantly, don't abuse this access to free and low cost materials or the institutions and organizations that are providing them. Everyone loses if the producers of these very valuable tools stop creating and disseminating them.

Resources in Your Area

Don't overlook potential sources of free or low-cost materials that may be available right in your own hometown. Here are a few examples of places to check. They might give you ideas for others as well. You should be able to find organizations or institutions like these listed in your local phone book.

The library is, of course, #1. Teachers have access to worlds of information from libraries. Tap into national clearinghouse resources, opportunities for on-line time with international electronic networks, free use of books, videos, films, and a myriad of other materials. Librarians can also help you with children's literature selections, what's popular, what works, etc.

The fire department. Most are affiliated with the national fire protection organizations and distribute a variety of materials on fire safety. Brochures and posters may be available, as well as professional fire fighters to give in-service presentations.

Local parks and recreation departments. Here's a good place for community-specific information about sports, local environmental issues, Earth Day celebrations, field trip possibilities, and more.

Local poison control centers. This is the place to go for Mr. Yuck stickers, brochures on poisonous substances, tips on what to do in an emergency, posters, and other materials to introduce kids to poison safety concepts.

Civic groups and church organizations. This could include Boy Scouts, Girl Scouts, Lions Clubs, Kiwanis, the local Junior Achievement people, YMCA, YWCA, League of Women Voters, Habitat for Humanity, or hundreds of other youth and community organizations. They may have posters, activities, brochures, information, or even famous members who can give presentations to your students.

City hall. If you want to know about the inner workings of your city, town, county, township, or municipality, there's no better source than city hall. Information on the structure of local government, how representatives are chosen, the history of the region, and much more is often available in a variety of formats.

Regional chapters of environmental groups. These can offer the kind of support services not always available from the national headquarters. Local and regional offices can often set up slide shows or other group presentations.

Hospitals and their outreach programs. Many of these offer a variety of health and diet related materials, posters, videos, booklets, and sometimes even experts who can augment audio-visual presentations.

Corporations. There are lots of big-name companies in this book that offer generous supplies of informational materials not only to their customers but also to the public at large, both as gestures of good citizenry, and as enlightened self-interest (for example, insurance companies promoting health or safety). Extensive corporate resources often produce top-quality teaching tools.

Universities or other institutions of higher learning. Though you may be teaching second graders, the local university or community college can provide curriculum ideas, contacts, or experts to share with your classes.

Museums and other cultural centers, symphonies, the theater, ballet, galleries, etc. You can get access to materials, special projects, field trips, traveling exhibitions, experts, audio-visual programs, and other educational aids that cannot be offered outside the institution's geographic region.

Sports teams. Local sports heroes make great inspirational speakers and are often available to talk with kids or give presentations.

State parks or recreation areas. These can be a wonderful source for a variety of materials about your regional history, geology, wildlife, and plant life.

Great Resources

The Smithsonian Institution is the largest museum complex in the world, with 16 main branches at the Washington headquarters filled with more than 140 million artifacts from every part of the globe. And that doesn't include the eight related galleries, archives, and research facilities in the New York area! If you want access to the more than 400 publications and other educational materials produced by the Smithsonian's many affiliates, the place to start is with the official *Smithsonian Resource Guide for Teachers*. The Office of Elementary and Secondary Education is responsible for compiling this 100-page directory. The staff there can also keep you up to date on the status of offered items and provide expert recommendations on what will best suit your students' needs. Listed resources include books, periodicals, comprehensive activity guides, dramatic audiovisual programs, posters, and more. Visual arts, performing arts, language arts, science, and social studies are represented. Also contains information on teaching aids from the Kennedy Center for the Performing Arts, the National Gallery of Art, and Reading is Fundamental!

Send: $5 (check or money order payable to the Smithsonian Institution)
Request: *The Smithsonian Resource Guide for Teachers*
Send to: Office of Elementary and Secondary Education
      Arts and Industries Building
      1163/MRC 402
      Smithsonian Institution
      Washington, DC 20560

Manipulatives and More

Clocks, blocks, counters, experiments, models, or activity books—if it has to do with mathematics, earth science, or physical science, Cuisenaire has an innovative product to suit the need. Famous for its math manipulatives, the 135-page catalog also includes an exclusive $16'' \times 21''$ full-color Cuisenaire poster illustrating a basic mathematical principle (past posters have tackled subjects such as statistical research, the geometry of quilts, and probability).

Send: Your name and address on school stationery
Or call: 1-800-237-3142
Request: The latest Cuisenaire catalog
Send to: Cuisenaire Company of America, Inc.
        10 Bank St.
        P.O. Box 5026
        White Plains, NY 10802

Budget Stretchers

Famous for engaging, giant floor puzzles, Frank Schaffer also offers hundreds of other budget-conscious products for the classroom. Here's the entire line of materials: math skill builders, language arts activities, workbooks for creative writing, charts, stickers, bulletin board sets, and more. Many items in this catalog cost under $5!

Send: Your name and address
Or call: 1-800-421-5565
Request: The latest Frank Schaffer catalog of teaching tools
Send to: Frank Schaffer Publications
        23740 Hawthorne Blvd.
        Torrance, CA 90505

Looking for the right textbook to implement your new geography curriculum? Or perhaps an on-line weather database, topographic map, or a board game about solutions to pollution? These five educational materials lists (15–20 pages each) can provide access to whatever you require. The lists are: *Textbooks, Map Product Sources and Publications, Software Materials, Games and Activities,* and *Environmental Information.*

Send: $5 (check or money order payable to the NCGE) for a set of five lists
Request: The complete collection of five resource lists
Send to: The National Council for Geographic Education
      16A Leonard Hall
      Indiana University of Pennsylvania
      Indiana, PA 15705-1087

MIDI Magic!

For those just beginning to explore the possibilities of musical instrument digital interface (MIDI), the *Music Technology Resource Guide for Educators* will provide invaluable assistance in comparing hardware, rating software, and evaluating curriculum needs. Those already involved with MIDI will appreciate the deeply discounted academic prices, software reviews, and technical advice.

Send: Your name and address
Or call: 1-800-348-5003
Request: *Music Technology Resource Guide for Educators*
Send to: Advanced Technologies
      19880 State Line Rd.
      South Bend, IN 46637

Consumer Power

Knowledge is power; teachers know that better than most. That's why this comprehensive guide to consumerism in America is a must-have for every household, rich or poor. The 125-page *Consumer's Resource Handbook* lists all the resources necessary to ensure an informed and effective buying public. This publication can provide endless ideas for activities revolving around economic, social, and environmental issues.

Send: Your name and address
Request: *Consumer's Resource Handbook*
Send to: Consumer's Resource Handbook
        Consumer Information Center
        Pueblo, CO 81009

Official Advice

You've seen the commercials, but have you taken advantage of this gold mine of information? Do! Discover hundreds of reports from national agencies, discussing everything from the best children's books (24 pages of info from the Literacy Council), to learning disabilities (40 pages from the National Institute of Mental Health), to the new food pyramid (30 pages from the USDA). Most are free; for others you'll pay postage fees ($.50 or $1).

Send: Your name and address
Or call: 719-948-4000
Request: The free *Consumer Information Catalog*
Send to: Consumer Information Catalog
        Pueblo, CO 81009

It takes two 30-page booklets just to explain how to access all the information available to you through the ERIC system, but here's a brief overview of why this is an unparalleled asset. More than 20 years ago the Educational Resources Information Center (ERIC) became the first commercial on-line database; it is now the largest education database in the world. ERIC contains more than 800,000 records of journal articles, research reports, curriculum guides, conference papers, and books. Each year 30,000 new records are added through the efforts of the 16 ERIC clearinghouses that collect, abstract, and index educational materials. ERIC can help answer any question you or your students have whether it regards trends in whole-language reading materials or additional details for a term paper on frog embryos. The ERIC system produces more than 250 publications each year so you can access all the latest research on high-interest topics. These publications are free or carry very nominal fees and include brochures, newsletters, pamphlets, bibliographies, curriculum guides, ideas for activities, and much more. The only way to really grasp the breadth of this resource is to see for yourself. These two directories are a great starting point.

Send: Your name and address
Or call: 1-800-LET-ERIC
Request: *All About ERIC* and
The ERIC Review
Send to: Access ERIC
       1600 Research Blvd.
       Rockville, MD 20850-3172

Aristo Fun!

The name comes from the Greek *aristos*, meaning "best," and what could be better than kids having fun while they learn? The AristoKids Club offers its exclusive newsletter filled with brain teasers, puzzles, experiments, and other activities, all reproducible for classroom use. The catalog of board games is filled with unique ideas for introducing complex subjects like archaeology in a very kid-friendly format.

Send: Your name and address
Request: AristoKids Club information and Aristoplay Catalog
Send to: Aristoplay
      P.O. Box 7028
      Ann Arbor, MI 48107

More than Maps

At the National Geographic Society, geography is far more than just flat images on topographic maps; it is, as proclaimed in the Society's mission statement, "... the description of land, sea, and universe...." The Society's Educational Services Catalog is a directory of hundreds of acclaimed documentary programs that an entire school district can use for years, plus lots of additional support services.

Send: Your name and address
Or call: 1-800-368-2728
Request: The NGS Educational Services Catalog
Send to: National Geographic Society
      P.O. Box 1269
      Washington, DC 20013-1269

Kid Time

Comparison shopping with classroom furnishing and sports equipment catalogs can give you the edge when it comes to purchasing necessary teaching tools. The Chime Time and Sport Time catalogs offer a full range of institutional-grade sports and classroom equipment, much of it manufactured exclusively for them using their own innovative designs.

Send: Your name and address
Or call: 1-800-477-5075 for Chime Time, 1-800-283-5700 for Sport Time
Request: The latest Chime Time or Sport Time catalogs
Send to: Chime Time
       2440-C Pleasantdale Rd.
       Atlanta, GA 30340-1562

Trendy Tools

In any profession, the right tools for the job make all the difference. Trend has a long-standing reputation for providing teachers with imaginative, colorful "tools" that engage students' attention and make learning fun! You've seen some of Trend's posters, room decor, stickers, flash cards, etc., in every supply catalog or store, but here's the entire collection, including the latest releases, directly from the source.

Send: Your name and address
Or call: 1-800-328-5540
Request: The latest Trend materials catalog
Send to: Trend Enterprises
       P.O. Box 64073
       St. Paul, MN 55164

Science Rules!

Need an articulated replica of the human skeleton? A comprehensive rock collection? Giant plywood models of dinosaurs? How about a simulated archaeological dig complete with pottery to restore? Everything you could want to spice up your science classroom is in this 112-page full-color wish book of endless experiments, test kits, models, specimen growing labs, and more. Big bang for small budgets from this source.

Send: Your name and address
Or call: 1-800-521-2832
Request: The Schoolmasters Science Catalog
Send to: Schoolmasters Science
      745 State Circle
      P.O. Box 1941
      Ann Arbor, MI 48106

Software Savings!

Software is the music that makes the blank computer screen sing. Unfortunately, amassing an inspiring variety of programs can cost big bucks. Shareware can help fill the gaps between your software budget and wish list, especially for those not yet on the "information super-highway." Try out programs *before* you buy and discover low-cost alternatives on subjects from pre-schooler skills to physics.

Send: Your name and address
Or call: 1-800-346-2842
Request: The free Shareware Express software catalog
Send to: Shareware Express
      1908-D Ashland St.
      Ashland, OR 97520

Looking for a guide to Capitol Hill and the process of law-making in America? A copy of the Congressional Record? Books on mathematics, earth science, solar energy, conservation, social sciences, or one of 150 other categories? Birds or insects? Oceanography? Music, language, global affairs? The United States Government Printing Office produces more than 12,000 books, periodicals, posters, pamphlets, and subscription services. Regardless of which entity created a publication, if it was a part of the federal government, its materials will be distributed by the Superintendent of Documents.

It takes a 16-page bibliography just to list and cross-reference the 150 categories of information covered. Using the *Subject Bibliography Index: A Guide to U.S. Government Publications*, choose your topic and request the catalog that contains ordering details for all related materials. Surprising values like 100-page books for a couple dollars are not uncommon. Three specialty catalogs offer direct access to items relevant to their themes. The Information for Business Catalog, New Products Catalog, and 95-page U.S. Subscriptions Catalog all list pamphlets, posters, teacher guides, and other educational aids. An immeasurable resource; target your interests or just browse for ideas!

Send: Your name and address
Request: The latest U.S. Government Subscriptions Catalog, Information for Business Catalog, New Products Catalog, and *Subject Bibliography Index*
Send to: The United States Government Printing Office
Superintendent of Documents
Washington, DC 20402

Theme Teaching

Building lesson plans around a central theme has proven an effective teaching technique because it supports a high level of interest from students. Theme teaching actually makes the educator's job simpler, since high-quality, developmentally appropriate thematic materials incorporate all curriculum agendas. This 20″ × 26″ chart cross-references hundreds of theme-based programs on the subjects of language arts, mathematics, social studies, and science.

Send: Your name and address on school stationery
Request: The poster chart *A Guide to Selecting and Organizing Books and Materials for Effective Theme Teaching in Grades K–8*
Send to: Sundance Publishing
234 Taylor St.
Littleton, MA 01460

Geography for Life

The nations of the planet are becoming more and more interconnected through the marvels of technologically advanced communications. Multicultural awareness, social tolerance, and geographic literacy are more important to students than ever. This 34-page executive summary can help with very specific standards for inspired geography instruction. Filled with beautiful photographs.

Send: $3 (check or money order payable to the NCGE)
Request: *Geography for Life Executive Summary: National Geography Standards*
Send to: The National Council for Geographic Education
16A Leonard Hall
Indiana University of Pennsylvania
Indiana, PA 15705-1087

Geo Standards

Geography as an investigatory discipline can be an exciting exploration for young minds, while it provides you with the means to correlate studies of both earth and social sciences. This 30-page guidebook to the enhanced standards for geographic competence describes the problems associated with geographic ignorance and delineates the fundamental principles of effective geography education. Very specific course objectives for every grade level.

Send: $3 (check or money order payable to the NCGE)
Request: *Guidelines for Geographic Education: Elementary and Secondary Schools*
Send to: The National Council for Geographic Education
16A Leonard Hall
Indiana University of Pennsylvania
Indiana, PA 15705-1087

Pre K–8 Review

Keep up on the very latest developments in the field of elementary education with the informative articles and teacher resources in *Teaching Pre K–8* magazine. Regular columns feature new books, education news, hi-tech in teaching, math, science, career advancement, and a monthly reproducible, plus guest commentary from the Secretary of Education. You can get a sample issue at no cost.

Send: Your name and address
Or call: 1-800-678-8793
Request: A sample preview issue of *Teaching Pre K–8*
Send to: Teaching Pre K–8
40 Richards Ave.
Norwalk, CT 06854

Teacher Training

Want to keep up on the latest developments in your field, share techniques and advice on handling everything from parental involvement to gang prevention, and explore ways to make your teaching more effective in all content areas? Don't miss this free annotated and illustrated listing of nearly 400 publications, videos, activity guides, and other curriculum materials.

Send: Your name and address
Or call: 1-800-995-4099
Request: The Educational Resources Catalog
Send to: California Department of Education
Publication Sales
P.O. Box 271
Sacramento, CA 95812-0271

Assessing Success

If you've ever wanted to make your testing and assessment practices more effective and useful for helping kids achieve their academic potential, check out the standards compiled by the National Education Association, the American Federation of Teachers, and the National Council on Measurement in Education. It's a detailed agenda for creating an assessment system that is fairer, more curriculum-specific, and more accurately reflective of students' achievements.

Send: Your name and address
Request: Standards for Teacher Competence in Educational Assessment of Students
Send to: National Council on Measurement in Education
1230 Seventeenth St. NW
Washington, DC 20036

Archaeology Assistance

How does the scientific pursuit of archaeology relate to Piagetian observations about a child's cognitive development? Can archaeology help your pupils enhance their critical observation or thinking skills? Explore all these questions and more in this information packet from the National Park Service.

Send: Your name and address on school stationery
Request: *Everything We Know About Archaeology for You to Use in Your Classroom*
Send to: U.S. Department of the Interior
National Park Service
Archaeological Assistance Program
P.O. Box 37127
Washington, DC 20013-7127

Grant Monies

Facilitate your search for funding to implement those innovative educational programs with the help of *Education Grants Alert*. This newsletter provides weekly updates on the availability of grant monies from both public and private sources, including eligibility requirements, deadlines for proposals, and a detailed examination of donors' goals. Ask for a free preview subscription.

Send: Your name and address
Or call: 1-800-655-5597
Request: The preview subscription to *Education Grants Alert*
Send to: Capitol Publications, Inc.
Education Grants Alert
1101 King St.
Alexandria, VA 22314

Global Pen Pals

Corresponding with children from other parts of the world is always an exciting experience for students and a great way to integrate a variety of subjects, such as language arts, history, culture, and geography. Where can you find kids to write to? Drop these groups a line and get your kids thinking globally!

American Association of Teachers of French
Bureau de Correspondence Scolaire
University of Illinois
59 East Armory Ave.
Champaign, IL 61820

Correspondence Agency for Students of French
College of Wooster
Wooster, OH 44691

International Friendship League
55 Mt. Vernon St., Beacon Hill
Boston, MA 02108

The League of Friendship
P.O. Box 509
Mount Vernon, OH 43050
(send a self-addressed stamped envelope)

Student Letter Exchange
910 Fourth St. SE
Austin, MN 55912

World Pen Pals
1694 Como Ave.
St. Paul, MN 55108

AFS Experience

Since 1947, AFS International has been promoting multi-cultural awareness through its student exchange network. Teens from 15 to 18 can experience firsthand the daily life of host families in 45 countries. More than just an opportunity to learn a second language, the adventure is often described by participants as profoundly life-changing. The *Host Family Scrapbook*'s colorful photographs and profiles tell the inside story. The AFS catalog describes programs and places around the world.

Send: Your name and address
Or call: 1-800-876-2377
Request: The latest AFS Programs Abroad catalog and *Host Family Scrapbook*
Send to: AFS Intercultural Programs USA
220 East 42nd St., 3rd Floor
New York, NY 10017-5806

Worthy Cause

Tired of the same old chocolate bar fundraisers? Want to make a statement while providing needed monies for trips and activities? American Environmental Outfitters offers a unique alternative with all-natural unbleached cotton T-shirts featuring earth-conscious messages silkscreened using environmentally safe methods and materials.

Send: Your name and address
Or call: 1-800-397-0292
Request: The AEO Fundraiser Kit
Send to: American Environmental Outfitters
242 Noble Rd.
Clarks Summit, PA 18411

With 18 million children in America currently affected by the divorce or separation of their parents, the potential pressures and emotional strain of stepfamily relations are a daily issue for many teachers. Such events can dramatically affect a student's ability to function in the classroom. The Stepfamily Association of America was founded in 1979 by doctors Emily and John Visher, after their own remarriage made them realize that there was a decided lack of psychological support services for newly united partners and their children. They have since revolutionized the concept of the stepparent, and nearly 20 years of research has resulted in a redefining of the roles each member of a "blended family" plays. Their work has helped thousands of people by exposing myths, misconceptions, and unrealistic expectations of stepfamily relations. Along with many books, published articles, and a quarterly newsletter, the SAA produces a comprehensive list of suggestions for educators that is carefully designed to assist you in ensuring that your classroom remains an encouraging and noncombative environment. It describes practical solutions for including all of a child's immediate family in school functions without conflict or placing innocent teachers in the middle of power struggles between former parental partners.

Send: Your name and address on school stationery
Request: *Support for Stepfamilies, Suggestions for Schools*
Send to: The Stepfamily Association of America, Inc.
215 Centennial Mall South, Suite 212
Lincoln, NE 68508

Sharing Humanity

Conduct a humane/environmental education workshop for your fellow teachers with the help of the *KIND Workshop Leader's Guide*. (KIND stands for Kids In Nature's Defense.) The booklet contains 30 pages of plans and discussion questions that will enable you to put on a one-hour, two-hour, or all-day seminar exploring the benefits of incorporating humane education in a school's curriculum. Includes detailed instructions for dozens of activities that can be duplicated in the classroom.

Send: $2.50 (check or money order payable to NAHEE)
Request: *KIND Workshop Leader's Guide*
Send to: The National Association for Humane and
      Environmental Education
      P.O. Box 362
      East Haddam, CT 06423-0362

Increasing Awareness

There are hundreds of publications, posters, videos, brochures, and other teaching aids in this 78-page catalog of materials available from the National Clearinghouse for Information. The subject is a tough one, drug abuse prevention, but all the tools are here to help you show kids satisfying alternatives to a dependent lifestyle and how they can find support for constructive personal choices.

Send: Your name and address
Or call: 1-800-729-6686
Request: The Information Publications Catalog
Send to: The Center for Substance Abuse Prevention
      National Clearinghouse for Information
      7079 Oakland Mills Rd.
      Columbia, MD 21046

Young readers have long expressed their desire for an information transfer medium that feels less intimidating than the traditional formal textbook. They want lively articles, interesting facts, engrossing pictorials, and opinions from all sides of an issue. You can give them that kind of excitement even when studying the sometimes dry dates and deeds of history with the help of the Cobblestone family of magazines. These periodicals present a wealth of information in a student-friendly format that allows the passion of people and events to come through. This 26-page full-color catalog discusses the complete Cobblestone line of magazines: *Odyssey*, which clarifies the mysteries of science for students in grades four through nine; *Calliope*, a comprehensive series on world history for grades five through ten; *Faces*, in-depth portraits of the varied cultures around the globe for grades four through nine; and the cornerstone magazine, *Cobblestone*, a portrait of American history from its earliest beginnings to the present, for grades four through nine. Cobblestone periodicals are compiled with the input of leading scientists, historians, museum personnel, and other experts who share their best work with students every month. Each issue also includes games, puzzles, extra activities, letters from readers, additional reading lists, and more.

Send: Your name and address
Or call: 1-800-821-0115
Request: The latest Cobblestone
Publishing catalog
Send to: Cobblestone Publishing, Inc.
7 School St.
Peterborough, NH 03458

Art & Music

Don't let inhibitions about your own singing or dancing expertise stop you from reaping the benefits of including musically oriented activities in the classroom. You can use music all through the school day: a familiar starting song that settles kids down, transition songs for changing the tempo to shift to a new activity, a closing song for the session's end. Music can be included to enhance dramatic play, language studies, and even math and can help students refine listening skills or learn to follow verbal directions. The addition of appropriate music often has its most dramatic impact on the level of enthusiastic participation in physical education activities.

This sampler tape and 24-page introductory workshop booklet contain more than 20 different playtime plans plus examples of accompanying songs. Lots of useful tips, how-tos, and classroom-tested techniques from the teaching professionals who are the authors of the curriculum suggestions. A comprehensive program with very specifically defined developmental goals appropriate for various ages.

Send: Your name and address
Or call: 1-800-631-2187
Request: The Kimbo Sampler Tape and Workshop Booklet
Send to: Kimbo Educational
          P.O. Box 477
          Long Branch, NJ 07740

Master the Music!

This master collection incorporates no less than seven different musical instrument and accessory sourcebooks from the Woodwind & the Brasswind family of catalogs. These represent the world's largest selection of musical instruments and their accessories at deeply discounted prices available only to teaching professionals.

Send: Your name and address
Or call: 1-800-348-5003
Request: The Master Catalog
Send to: The Woodwind & The Brasswind
19880 State Line Rd.
South Bend, IN 46637

Performance Props

Whatever your needs—be they costumes, makeup, lighting, or others—if it has to do with the technical behind-the-scenes work of a theatrical production, the *Performing Arts Buyers Guide* can direct you to the source. Ninety-six pages of instructional and reference materials deal with film, theater, and dance. This resource includes books, videos, and information on everything from cut-out dolls of famous ballerinas to instructions for staging a sword fight. No minimum order size.

Send: Your name and address
Or call: 1-800-523-0961
Request: The latest issue of the *Performing Arts Buyers Guide*
Send to: The Performing Arts Buyers Guide
Stagestep
P.O. Box 328
Philadelphia, PA 19105

You've seen the effects that well-chosen music can have on a classroom—setting a mood or calming restless kids. Beyond its established ability to enhance brain function, when children make the music themselves it's a powerful tool for teaching a variety of useful skills, including eye-hand coordination, spatial or tonal discrimination, following directions, even reading and group cooperation. Rhythm Band is the world's largest manufacturer of elementary musical instruments and can offer products to help you inexpensively outfit your students with a wide range of beginner equipment that will allow the whole class to participate in music activities. It's a complete selection of easy-to-play percussion-type instruments: drums, bells, triangles, cymbals, castanets, and the like. This catalog offers access to everything from authentic ethnic artifacts such as the Hawaiian uli uli or an African axatse (the first a bead-filled gourd decorated with brilliant red feathers, the latter a giant gourd covered with a vibrating beaded net), to the simplest ankle bells, spoons, or slit log drums. Dozens of items priced at around $5: recorders, harmonicas, triangles, plus song books, note charts, and other music accessories. The 44-page full-color catalog also has helpful tips for choosing instruments.

Send: Your name and address
Or call: 1-800-424-4724
Request: The latest Rhythm Band Instruments catalog
Send to: Rhythm Band Instruments
      P.O. Box 126
      Fort Worth, TX 76101-0126

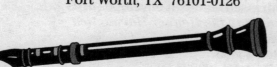

French Impressionism

Along with its many other masterpieces, the Art Institute
of Chicago has amassed a particularly impressive collection of works from French artists of the Impressionist and
Post-Impressionist periods. This set of ten full-color postcards ($5'' \times 7''$ size, many with explanatory text), brings the
most famous of those works right into your classroom for
students to examine and discuss.

Send: $2.50 (check or money order payable to Teacher
Programs; include your name, address, school name, and
phone numbers)
Request: Postcard Packs: *Impressionism*
Send to: Teacher Resource Center
        The Art Institute of Chicago
        111 South Michigan Ave.
        Chicago, IL 60603-6110

Harmonica Harmony

Enthusiasts proclaim it to be the most economical, com-
pact, easy-to-learn musical instrument ever invented. The
harmonica has certainly had its share of famous fans,
from Abraham Lincoln to Ronald Reagan. Even the
youngest students can learn to play the *mund-aeoline*
(German for "mouth harp"), especially with the aid of this
24-page instruction booklet. Includes techniques, songs,
tips for choosing the right harmonicas, and some harmonica history.

Send: A self-addressed stamped envelope (#10)
Request: *How to Play the Hohner Harmonica*
Send to: Hohner, Inc.
        P.O. Box 15035
        Richmond, VA 23227-5035

American Art Heritage

It was a time of gigantic canvases filled with richly textured landscapes, stylized scenes of daily life, vibrant impressions of the age. Introduce your students to the great American artists who left their unique mark on the world of painting with this set of 16 full-color postcards (5"×7" size, most with accompanying text), including famous works from the likes of Homer, Remington, and others.

Send: $4 (check or money order payable to Teacher Programs; include your name, address, school name, and phone numbers)
Request: Postcard Packs: *Art from North America*
Send to: Teacher Resource Center
The Art Institute of Chicago
111 South Michigan Ave.
Chicago, IL 60603-6110

English Elegance

Too many students will never have the opportunity to visit the world's great museums, but you can bring some of the finest artistic works from all the ages directly to them with archival art prints from the British Museum. Thirty black-and-white, 5"×8", quality prints present paintings, sculpture, and other media molded by the masters.

Send: $3.50 (check or money order payable to The University Prints)
Request: *Visits to Great Museums: The British Museum in London*
Send to: The University Prints
21 East St.
P.O. Box 485
Winchester, MA 01890

America's National Gallery of Art is home to one of the world's leading museum collections. Its art appreciation tours use subjects like the senses, families, and color to bring art to kids as young as four. Special topic tours go more in-depth for kids in grades four through 12 and coordinate various art forms with subjects like history, literature, math, science, and creative writing.

But the exciting part is that you don't have to live near Washington, D.C., to make good classroom use of this inspiring national treasure. The Gallery of Art encourages teachers everywhere to take advantage of its generous extension program, which allows educators to request color slide presentations, films, video cassettes, video laser discs, and even complete curriculum packs (booklets, color slides, study prints, and a time line of art history), to use, free of charge, for a full week. Students can study portraiture through paintings of famous people, European or American masterworks, or the entire history and collections of the National Gallery itself. There are hundreds of valuable extension programs to choose from, and the 40-page catalog is the guide to it all, including how to register for the materials that best integrate with your curriculum.

Send: Your name and address
Or call: 202-842-6263
Request: National Gallery of Art
Extension Programs catalog
Send to: Department of Education
　　　　　Resources
　　　　　Extension Programs Section
　　　　　National Gallery of Art
　　　　　Washington, DC 20565

Ancient Artistry

Ever since early *Homo sapiens* experimented with self-expression through charcoal drawings on a cave wall, animals have been one of the favorite subjects for human beings' artistic endeavors. From prehistoric stick figures to the intricately authentic details of the Renaissance naturalist painters, this 50-page guide provides interesting facts, photos, engravings, and hands-on activities for exploring the subject of animals in art!

Send: $4.50 (check or money order payable to Cobblestone Publishing)
Request: #F1995-01: *Faces Magazine: Animals in Art*
Send to: Cobblestone Publishing, Inc.
7 School St.
Peterborough, NH 03458

Chicago Art

Take your class on a customized tour through the Art Institute of Chicago's truly extensive collection of world-renowned paintings and sculptures without ever leaving the comfort of home. This 18-page directory of the Institute's materials lists filmstrips, videos, a complete teacher resource center for advice on all aspects of art and your curriculum, plus free software on seven art topics (you pay only for the discs).

Send: Your name and address
Request: The latest Student/Teacher Programs catalog
Send to: Teacher Resource Center
The Art Institute of Chicago
111 South Michigan Ave.
Chicago, IL 60603-6110

Paris Rendezvous

Whisk students off to the romance and history of France's art without leaving the classroom! This packet of fine art prints features works of the great European artists from the last several centuries, part of the collection at the Louvre Museum in Paris. Thirty different black-and-white art prints (5″ × 8″ size) of masterpieces.

Send: $3.50 (check or money order payable to The University Prints)
Request: *Visits to Great Museums: Paris, the Louvre*
Send to: The University Prints
        21 East St.
        P.O. Box 485
        Winchester, MA 01890

European Artistry

The Art Institute of Chicago maintains one of the world's most comprehensive collections of art masterpieces. But you don't have to live nearby to make use of the museum's remarkable resources. This set of 16 full-color 5″ × 7″ postcards with accompanying text brings you a selection of the Art Institute's better-known pieces from the European continent: paintings, furniture, textiles, and period miniatures. Great visual aids.

Send: $4 (check or money order payable to Teacher Programs; include your name, address, school name, and phone numbers)
Request: Postcard Packs: *Art from Europe*
Send to: Teacher Resource Center
        The Art Institute of Chicago
        111 South Michigan Ave.
        Chicago, IL 60603-6110

Leather Lore

Leathercraft can assure young students a satisfying first experience working with their hands. Tandy group kits or individual projects come in dozens of designs, providing inexpensive ways to supply your craft class with everything they need for easy construction and surefire results. Prices start as low as $.49 per project. The catalog lists stores in your area that offer free leathercraft demonstrations to schools and other student groups.

Send: Your name and address
Request: The latest leather products catalog
Send to: Tandy Leather
P.O. Box 791
Fort Worth, TX 76101

Supply Side Savings

It's hard to express your artistry without adequate supplies, and every teacher knows how much those can end up costing. Saving 30 percent or more on materials means being able to inspire young artists while staying within the budget. Suncoast Discount Arts and Crafts can help with a complete selection of art supplies: paints, parts, patterns, all the raw materials you need for a classroom full of creative fun.

Send: Your name and address
Or fax: 813-571-1182
Request: The latest discount art and craft supplies catalogs
Send to: Suncoast Discount Arts and Crafts
4682 107th Circle North
Clearwater, FL 34622

Fiber Facts

Enliven your craft classes with some excursions into the fiber arts, even if you don't know your soda ash from your batik resists. The Dharma Trading Company catalog shares 25 years of experience and offers an extensive selection of inexpensive raw materials. The 115-page guide also includes a wealth of specific tips and techniques to take you from proper fabric preparation through easy clean-up.

Send: Your name and address
Or call: 1-800-542-5227
Request: The latest Dharma Trading Company catalog
Send to: Dharma Trading Company
P.O. Box 150916
San Rafael, CA 94915

All that Glitters

Add some dazzle to even the most basic crafts projects with this assortment of glitter. Great for those glue and glitter drawings that kids love (draw a design with regular white glue, generously sprinkle glitter all over the glue, pour off excess into a container to use again!). This introductory packet contains eight tubes of glitter: orange, gold, red, green, blue, white, silver, and mixed.

Send: $4.75 (check or money order payable to Treasure Toy House)
Or call: 1-800-328-0084
Request: #B-206: Tubes of Glitter
Send to: Treasure Toy House, Inc.
6010 Lone Oak Rd.
P.O. Box 58
Rockford, MN 55373

Health & Safety

Long regarded as the most respected source for advice on the latest developments in child care, the American Academy of Pediatrics offers a variety of valuable informational materials. Request brochures by name. Individual samples of the assorted brochures are available at no cost. Titles include: *Growing Up Healthy: Fat, Cholesterol and More; Right from the Start: ABC's of Good Nutrition for Young Children; Playground Safety; TV and the Family;* and *Choking Prevention and First Aid for Infants and Children.* You can also query the Academy about other ongoing public information projects and safety videos for kids on topics such as bike helmets and handling emergency situations.

Send: A self-addressed stamped envelope
Request: The brochure by name
Send to: American Academy of Pediatrics
　　　　Department C: (title of brochure)
　　　　P.O. Box 927
　　　　Elk Grove Village, IL
　　　　60009-0927

Team Nutrition

The USDA's Food and Nutrition Service has compiled a year's worth of clever ideas to help educators instill in their pupils the basics of why it's important to choose wholesome, nutritious foods. A 12-month calendar displays facts, tips, and food-related activities that support healthy eating habits. Send this important message home with the "10 Steps to Healthy Eating" refrigerator magnet and parent's guide, also included.

Send: Your name and address on school stationery
Request: The Healthy Kids Teacher Information Pack
Send to: The USDA's Team Nutrition
Food and Nutrition Service
3103 Park Center Dr., Room 802
Alexandria, VA 22302-1594

Food Groups

Even primary-grade kids can grasp the basic five food group concept and begin to understand the importance of supplying their bodies with wholesome, effective fuel. The whimsical drawings on this full-color poster depict kids making healthy food choices. On its back side, the 25″× 33″ poster has a discussion of daily servings and why we eat food.

Send: $3 (check or money order payable to the National Dairy Council)
Request: #0505N: *Eat the Five Food Group Way!* poster
Send to: The National Dairy Council
10255 West Higgins Rd., Suite 900
Rosemont, IL 60018-5616

Pyramid Power

The daily food guide pyramid offers a specific standard for evaluating the components of a healthy, balanced diet. This 26"×35" pyramid poster features colorful photos of breads, vegetables, fruits, meats, and more, bringing each of the five food groups into perspective for students and providing easy reference on the appropriate variety and serving size of daily fare. The back discusses combination foods and that "others" category.

Send: $4 (check or money order payable to the National Dairy Council)
Request: #0502N: *Daily Food Guide Pyramid* poster
Send to: The National Dairy Council
          10255 West Higgins Rd., Suite 900
          Rosemont, IL 60018-5616

Nutrition Alert!

You've seen them in the national media, exposing food *faux pas* in chain restaurants and movie theaters. Now your class can be among the first to learn about the Center for Science in the Public Interest's ongoing activities through its enlightening *Nutrition Action Healthletter*. Discover the secrets of the ten foods you should never eat, what's behind the hype on sport drinks, vitamins, "low-fat," and more. You can receive a sample issue for free.

Send: Your name and address on school stationery
Request: A sample issue of *Nutrition Action Healthletter*
Send to: The Center for Science in the Public Interest
          1875 Connecticut Ave. NW, Suite 300
          Washington, DC 20009-5728

Building Better Bodies

Unlike teenage girls, boys are often most concerned with gaining weight, specifically, adding muscle. This 25-page guide to fitness for young men examines the important role that wholesome food can play in building strong, agile, healthy bodies. Includes ten techniques for increasing endurance, the real reasons to exercise, vitamin facts, plus answers to questions about sports and how performance can be linked to nutrition.

Send: $3 (check or money order payable to the National Dairy Council)
Request: A copy of *You! Your Guide to Food, Fitness and Fun!: for Young Men*
Send to: The National Dairy Council
　　　　10255 West Higgins Rd., Suite 900
　　　　Rosemont, IL 60018-5616

Cleanliness Counts

This packet of information was specifically designed to help educators give children a clear understanding of why cleanliness is so important to both our public and personal health. Cartoons and full-color mini-posters depict the kinds of activities that definitely require handwashing afterwards. A cassette is included, featuring the *Hooray for Handwashing* story starring Soapy and Sudsy, along with simple handwashing songs for young students.

Send: $5 (check or money order payable to the Soap and Detergent Association)
Request: *The ABC's of Clean* classroom packet
Send to: The Soap and Detergent Association
　　　　475 Park Ave. South
　　　　New York, NY 10016

The youth of America have been participating in the President's Physical Fitness Programs since 1966. Nearly 28,000 schools nationwide are currently involved in the movement, with more than 2.5 million awards being distributed each year. The two newest prizes are the *Presidential Physical Fitness Award* for outstanding achievement and the *Participant Physical Fitness Award*. The latter insures that all children who at least attempt the challenge will receive some kind of acknowledgment of their efforts. Any student from six to 17 (including those with special needs) can get involved in these programs. The introductory packet contains all the materials needed to start your class or school down the road to physical health and well-being. On a colorful 17″×22″ poster, Challenge co-chairs Tom McMillen and Florence Griffith Joyner encourage kids to "Get Moving." The 40-page *Get Fit Handbook* is filled with practice exercises to get kids ready for the specific physical requirements and explanations of the five components of the Challenge tests. Also included are a letter from the President, entry forms for the State Champion titles, a testing manual, and scorecards that allow tracking of test results over a period of years.

Send: Your name and address on school stationery
Or call: 1-800-258-8146
Request: The introductory informational packet on the President's Physical Fitness Challenge Programs
Send to: The President's Challenge
Poplars Research Center
400 East 7th St.
Bloomington, IN 47405

Food, Fitness, Fun

Teenage girls often have an ambiguous relationship with food. This colorful 25-page guide to health and fitness offers expert advice for girls on subjects like sensible snacking and working out. It also touches on difficult issues such as eating disorders and body image, then provides practical tips on exercise, calculating calories in vs. calories out, and monitoring body fat.

Send: $3 (check or money order payable to the National Dairy Council)
Request: A copy of *You! Your Guide to Food, Fitness and Fun!: for Young Women*
Send to: The National Dairy Council
10255 West Higgins Rd., Suite 900
Rosemont, IL 60018-5616

Fast Food Facts

Middle, junior, and high school students find themselves increasingly responsible for making their own decisions about what to consume for snacks, and often full meals. Show them the healthier alternatives that are available even at their favorite fast food restaurants. This eight-page brochure provides food values for fried chicken, burgers, pizza, tacos, and more, as well as nutritious 500-calorie meals and diet basics. Enough for the whole class.

Send: $5 (check or money order payable to the National Dairy Council)
Request: 20 copies of #0135N: *Fast Food: Today's Guide to Healthy Choices*
Send to: The National Dairy Council
10255 West Higgins Rd., Suite 900
Rosemont, IL 60018-5616

Fire Safety Friend

Since 1896 the National Fire Protection Association has been providing support services for education on fire safety–related issues. The Association's complete 92-page catalog lists dozens of informative brochures, posters, and other visual aids, along with lesson plans and activity guides for teachers. Captivate and educate your younger students with the Sparky the Firehouse Hound hand puppets (package of 30 just $2.75).

Send: Your name and address
Or call: 1-800-344-3555
Request: The classroom pack of Sparky puppets and/or the National Fire Protection Association catalog
Send to: The National Fire Protection Association
P.O. Box 9101
Quincy, MA 02269-9101

Smoke Detectives

This fire safety education program provides weeks of interrelated subject matter to explore. The hefty notebook contains a 25-minute video, full-color poster, lesson plans, activity sheets, reproducibles, and special projects to involve the entire school. For grades K through six.

Send: Your name, address, phone number, and school name
Request: The *Smoke Detectives* Classroom Kit
Send to: Smoke Detectives
Public Relations Department
State Farm Insurance Companies
One State Farm Plaza
Bloomington, IL 61710-0001

Did you know that nearly every 90 minutes somewhere in the United States a train and a motor vehicle collide? In 1993 there were nearly 5,000 such railroad crossing accidents, hundreds of them fatal, all of them preventable if the drivers had only used some simple common sense. You can help your students develop the awareness needed to keep them from ever becoming one of these sad statistics with the various materials available through Operation Lifesaver. The national Operation Lifesaver headquarters will direct you to your individual state's Program Coordinator who can then provide you with a wealth of brochures and informational publications useful in promoting train safety. Older kids can check their current driving habits against the "Can You Make the Grade?" quiz that discusses all the rules of the road regarding trains. Younger children can get a good head start on developing their knowledge of train safety with *The Operation Lifesaver Coloring Book.* Through it children are encouraged to respect the power of trains and never take chances around them. Your state coordinator can provide you with coloring books for your entire class as well as arrange for other in-school train safety programs.

Send: Your name and address
Or call: 1-800-537-6224
Request: *The Operation Lifesaver Coloring Book*
Send to: Operation Lifesaver
        1522 King St.
        Alexandria, VA 22314

Water Wise

Amazingly, just *part* of an average day for the U.S. Coast Guard consists of saving 15 lives, assisting 330 people to safety, saving 1.5 million dollars in property, and responding to 34 pollutant spills. The Coast Guard also dispenses volumes of information on safe boating practices. Lots of interesting maritime facts and discussion topics.

Send: Your name and address
Or call: 1-800-368-5647
Request: Safe Boating Information Packet
Send to: Customer Service (G-NAB)
U.S. Coast Guard Headquarters
2100 Second St. SW
Washington, DC 20593-0001

Movers & Shakers

Could an earthquake happen in your region? Would your class be prepared? This well-rounded program explains plate tectonics and what causes earthquakes. It also illustrates proper emergency procedures to follow if an earthquake were to occur. Adaptable for use with students K through 12. The sturdy notebook contains a 25-minute video, teacher's guide, lesson plans, ideas for activities, reproducibles, and a two-sided full-color poster!

Send: Your name, address, phone number, and school name
Request: The *Movers & Shakers* Classroom Kit
Send to: Movers & Shakers
Public Relations Department
State Farm Insurance Companies
One State Farm Plaza
Bloomington, IL 61710-0001

Positive Peer Pressure

It takes more than mere lectures, parental pleading, or even municipal ordinances to get children to comprehend the fragility of the human form and willingly, faithfully wear their helmets or other protective sporting gear. What's required is a community-wide effort to make safety consciousness "cool." This 15-page booklet gives detailed how-tos for creating three community-interactive Head-Smart events specifically designed to do just that.

Send: $3.50 (check or money order payable to the National Head Injury Foundation)
Request: Item #2: *The HeadSmart Schools Guideline Packet for Community Involvement*
Send to: The National Head Injury Foundation
HeadSmart Program
Attention: Materials and Publications
1776 Massachusetts Ave. NW, Suite 100
Washington, DC 20036

Playground Safety

Though this special safety checklist was designed for use by parents to help them evaluate the play areas their own children frequent, it also has tremendous value for teachers. With more than 150,000 children each year receiving emergency-room treatment for playground equipment–related injuries, it's a valid concern to everyone with an interest in kids' welfare.

Send: A self-addressed stamped envelope
Request: Parent's Playground Checklist
Send to: Consumer Federation of America
1424 16th St. NW, Suite 604
Washington, DC 20036-2211

Eye Alert

Good eyesight is critical to a child's ability to function in the classroom. This brochure from Prevent Blindness America will help you boost your knowledge of the most common eye problems suffered by children and learn the most obvious signs indicating potential problems.

Send: Your name and address
Or call: 1-800-331-2020
Request: *Signs of Possible Eye Trouble in Children* brochure
Send to: The National Society to Prevent Blindness
Educational Materials
500 East Remington Rd.
Schaumburg, IL 60173

Helmet Pride

Each year 50,000 bicycle riders suffer serious head trauma injuries, the vast majority of which could be prevented by use of a helmet. This HeadSmart coloring and activity book starts kids off right with a healthy attitude about wearing their protective gear. Cartoons to color, a puzzle maze, the Be Smart mask, plus tips for helmet use. Enough of the eight-page booklets for a whole class.

Send: $5 (check or money order payable to the National Head Injury Foundation)
Request: Item #7, 20 count: *The HeadSmart Activity Book*
Send to: The National Head Injury Foundation
HeadSmart Program
Attention: Materials and Publications
1776 Massachusetts Ave. NW, Suite 100
Washington, DC 20036

Shell Sense

"You're Not Born With It" is the message of this $17'' \times 22''$ two-color public service announcement poster from the National Head Injury Foundation. It reminds kids that they don't have personal armor plating like that of a turtle and offers an engaging way to illustrate the need for protective safety equipment. Kids tend to appreciate this commonsense view of why helmets are so important.

Send: $1
Request: Item #8: *You're Not Born With It* poster
Send to: The National Head Injury Foundation
HeadSmart Program
Attention: Materials and Publications
1776 Massachusetts Ave. NW, Suite 100
Washington, DC 20036

Eyes and Sports

Fully half of all blindness is preventable with proper care and consideration for the safety of the eyes. Use of eye protection during sports activities is one of the easiest ways to make a substantial reduction in the number of accidental eye injuries that occur each year, many of which can be permanently disabling. Create an atmosphere where safety is an accepted priority and protective eyewear is standard equipment.

Send: Your name and address
Or call: 1-800-331-2020
Request: *Don't Play Games with Your Eyes* brochure
Send to: The National Society to Prevent Blindness
Educational Materials
500 East Remington Rd.
Schaumburg, IL 60173

Head Smarts

Programs like HeadSmart have had a tremendous impact on reducing the incidence of head trauma injuries in kids. HeadSmart stickers can help encourage safety consciousness in your class and make wearing protective gear the accepted thing to do! You get a nice supply: 40 peel-back stickers, bright 2½" circles with a red helmet on a large smiley face that says "HeadSmart."

Send: $4.80 (check or money order payable to the National Head Injury Foundation)
Request: Item #4, 40 count: HeadSmart Stickers
Send to: The National Head Injury Foundation
HeadSmart Program
Attention: Materials and Publications
1776 Massachusetts Ave. NW, Suite 100
Washington, DC 20036

Violence Prevention

There are resources for fire prevention, drug abuse prevention, child abuse prevention, etc. This catalog's materials are geared toward helping educators prevent violence in their schools. The lesson plans concentrate on teaching children practical skills to help them deal constructively with the inevitable conflicts of life. Kids learn how to effectively communicate, negotiate, and mediate their differences rather than resort to aggression.

Send: Your name and address
Request: The Resources for Empowering Children catalog
Send to: Educators for Social Responsibility
23 Garden St.
Cambridge, MA 02138

Inside Out

This kit helps instill in young students the basic concepts of personal health and well-being. For use in grades K through six. Comes with a hardcover notebook, 25-minute animated video, comic books, lesson plans, ideas for related activities, and reproducibles.

Send: Your name, address, phone number, and school name
Request: The *Inside/Out* Classroom Kit
Send to: Inside/Out
       Public Relations Department
       State Farm Insurance Companies
       One State Farm Plaza
       Bloomington, IL 61710-0001

Thought, Word, Deed

Endorsed by the National Association of Elementary School Principals, the American School Counselors Association, and the Character Counts! Coalition, this program relates reading, writing, and personal action to show students how to become responsible, thoughtful citizens of their communities. Contains a 25-minute video, a notebook with lesson plans, supporting activities, and reproducibles. For all grades.

Send: Your name, address, phone number, and school name
Request: The *Thought Word & Deed* Classroom Kit
Send to: Thought Word & Deed
       Public Relations Department
       State Farm Insurance Companies
       One State Farm Plaza
       Bloomington, IL 61710-0001

Life Skills

This large notebook of materials contains a model curriculum that covers all the grades from K through 12. It presents a comprehensive program developed by the U.S. Department of Education to assist teachers in creating individual courses that will reach students with the message of living free from drug dependence. Activities, teacher tips, and background information stress strong life skills and good information as a kid's best defense.

Send: Your name and address
Or call: 1-800-729-6686
Request: *Learning to Live Drug Free: A Curriculum Model for Prevention*
Send to: The Center for Substance Abuse Prevention
National Clearinghouse for Information
7079 Oakland Mills Rd.
Columbia, MD 21046

SADD

Don't let the name set the mood; this organization's message is about conscious living, not melancholy. The SADD motto states: "In the effort to save young lives, the only losers are those who don't bother to try!" The educator kit contains everything you need to put together a variety of activities that support kids in making responsible life choices.

Send: Your name, school, and school address
Request: The SADD Educator Awareness Kit
Send to: Students Against Drunk Driving
P.O. Box 8702
Clinton, IA 52736-8702

Social Studies

Spice up that mythology unit with some photos of authentic Greek and Roman sculptures; spark an interest in ancient history by presenting actual portraits of medieval noblemen; take kids into Egyptian pyramids, through the Italian renaissance, into the castles of Europe. Anywhere and everywhere humans have left their art, it's cataloged and accessible through this extensive archive of photo prints. Founded nearly 90 years ago, the University Prints collection is one of the most comprehensive in the world, reproducing works held by every well-known museum.

This "visual archive of art history" offers more than 7,500 photos (with captions) of people, places, and things stretching to the beginnings of civilization, from every part of the globe. Three hundred prints of famous paintings are available in color; the rest of the archive's materials are all standard $5'' \times 8''$, black and white art prints on heavy paper stock. (Color prints are $.15 each, black and white $.08.) You can select individual prints to be custom bound or sent to you in loose-leaf collections. Sample prints are available upon request to assist teachers in preparing their own "visual textbooks."

Send: $4 (check or money order payable to The University Prints)
Request: The University Prints Complete Catalog
Send to: The University Prints
21 East St.
P.O. Box 485
Winchester, MA 01890

Queen of the Nile

Step into the exotic world of Bellerophon, where ancient history meets artistic creativity in the unlikely form of a coloring book. Within this unique format you'll find an astonishing wealth of historical information from the art to the structure of ancient societies! Endless ideas for further studies and a great way to introduce kids to difficult subjects. Learn about Cleopatra here, then request the complete catalog of materials!

Send: $4.50 (check or money order payable to Bellerophon Books; CA residents add appropriate sales tax)
Request: #175-6: *A Coloring Book of Cleopatra*
Send to: Bellerophon Books
        36 Anacapa St.
        Santa Barbara, CA 93101

Holy Crusaders

Here's an in-depth study of the Crusades of the Middle Ages that even includes a firsthand account from the daughter of Byzantine Emperor Alexius II describing the knights invading the city of Constantinople. Fifty pages of photos, engravings, detailed articles, a map of the Crusades, a timeline of events, plus instructions for related activities.

Send: $4.50 (check or money order payable to Cobblestone Publishing)
Request: #C1995-01: *Calliope Magazine: The First Crusades*
Send to: Cobblestone Publishing, Inc.
7 School St.
Peterborough, NH 03458

When in Rome

Look out through the pillars of the Acropolis, stand amidst the ruins of the Coliseum, let students wonder at the artistic and architectural marvels of an ancient world. This set of 30 art prints (black and white, 5″ × 8″ size) from the National Museum in Athens helps bring life to historical texts and illuminate an influential age. Integrate reading skills, history, geography, culture, and more.

Send: $3.50 (check or money order payable to The University Prints)
Request: *Visits to Great Museums: The National Museum at Athens*
Send to: The University Prints
21 East St.
P.O. Box 485
Winchester, MA 01890

Zeus Lives!

Was that Helena or Athena? What oracle? Is he Zeus or Poseidon? Connect real statues, ancient architectural wonders, and paintings of various gods with the written stories of classical mythology and help students better relate the legends they're learning to an actual period in human history. This 30-card set of fine art prints (5″ × 8″ size) depicts the best-known myths and figures (with captions).

Send: $3.50 (check or money order payable to The University Prints)
Request: *Classical Mythology: Gods and Goddesses*
Send to: The University Prints
           21 East St.
           P.O. Box 485
           Winchester, MA 01890

Diplomacy and Money

This 105-page guide presents, then answers a series of intriguing, globally relevant questions for your upper-grade students to ponder and research. What is the World Bank? The International Monetary Fund? What is the United Nations Security Council and how can it influence the way governments conduct their affairs? What does imposing economic sanctions mean? Lots of historical references, and the basis for great essay questions.

Send: Your name and address on school stationery
Request: A copy of *Image & Reality—Questions and Answers About the United Nations*
Send to: Public Inquiries Unit
　　　　　 Public Services Section
　　　　　 Department of Public Information
　　　　　 The United Nations
　　　　　 New York, NY 10017

Global Village

Enhance a geography or world cultures unit with a lesson on flags of the world. You can discuss flag symbolism, national pride, how flags change through history, and much more. These gummed labels show the flags of 200 countries. They can be used as a whole sheet or separated for passing around.

Send: $3.50 (check or money order payable to the Jamestown Stamp Company)
Request: #Y-720: 200 Flags of the World
Send to: Jamestown Stamp Company
　　　　　 341 East Third St.
　　　　　 Jamestown, NY 14701-0019

Powers That Be

Though constantly changing political entities present quite a challenge for the geopolitical mapmakers, they also provide fertile ground for classroom activities relating the cultural, social, geographic, or economic identities of countries and exploring the roots of upheaval. A 22″× 40″color Geological Survey map depicting the capitals and political situation of every country can help.

Send: $3.75 (check or money order payable to U.S. Geological Survey)
Request: *Political Map of the World*
Send to: Branch of Distribution
U.S. Geological Survey
Box 25286, Federal Center
Denver, CO 80225

Fair Trade

Here's a unique window to indigenous peoples and cultures around the world that's sure to leave a lasting impression on students. The 20-minute video (free on loan) and SERRV poster explain how global, grassroots fair trade networks with native populations can enrich the lives of the handcrafts producers and the consumers.

Send: Your name and address
Or fax: 410-635-8774
Request: The teacher information kit with video and poster
Send to: SERRV Handcrafts
500 Main St.
P.O. Box 365
New Windsor, MD 21776-0365

Nations United

The topic encompasses history, language, geography, war, and peace. Introduce your middle-grade students to the United Nations with this 25-page guide. An age-appropriate discussion of the UN's beginnings, the reasons for its formation, its intended mission, the official languages used at the UN village, the internal structure of the governing bodies, and how each country plays a role in the assemblage. Pop quiz included.

Send: Your name and address on school stationery
Request: A copy of *What's the United Nations?*
Send to: Public Inquiries Unit
Public Services Section
Department of Public Information
The United Nations
New York, NY 10017

Discovering Deutschland

Here's an example to illustrate the values you can find at the consulates and information services listed in the countries index in this chapter. A friendly request to the German information bureau resulted in an astonishing array of usable materials: books, maps, periodicals, pamphlets, and posters exploring every detail of German geography, culture, history, politics, and economics both in English and German. Endless ideas for activities.

Send: Your name and address on school stationery
Request: General or specific information about Germany and its people, depending on your needs
Send to: The German Information Center
950 Third Ave.
New York, NY 10022-2781

Global Village

The UN Plaza is a historic site, home to delegates from around the world, its structures cooperatively designed by architects from many nations. This 20-page guide to the UN complex describes each building in exacting detail. Great ideas for many projects.

Send: Your name and address on school stationery
Request: Press Feature #217: *United Nations Headquarters*
Send to: Public Inquiries Unit
Public Services Section
Department of Public Information
The United Nations
New York, NY 10017

Peacekeepers

It seems like UN Peacekeepers are in the news every day, deployed to help countries and people in need. What's their mission? Who decides where and when they will be sent? Where do they come from? Answers to these questions and many more are discussed on the back of this 24″ × 20″ full-color poster. The front is comprised of photos of the UN Secretary General and troops fulfilling their missions of peace.

Send: Your name and address on school stationery
Request: *Peacekeeping: Answers at Your Fingertips* poster
Send to: Public Inquiries Unit
Public Services Section
Department of Public Information
The United Nations
New York, NY 10017

Affairs of State

The autographed $8'' \times 10''$ color glossy of the Secretary of State is, in itself, a nice jumping off point for discussions on the structure of government, current international news, U.S. politics, etc. But you can also tap into events as they transpire around the world through the State Department's daily press briefings and fact sheets on diplomatic endeavors.

Send: Your name and address
Request: The Public Information Series introductory packet
Send to: The U.S. Department of State
Bureau of Public Affairs
Washington, DC 20520

Rebels with a Cause

Students in the secondary grades are no strangers to the desire for rebellion, which makes this 40-page booklet a great tool for teaching about history, culture, politics, and reform. The populist, civil rights, and environmental movements are discussed in detail. Included are historical photos, personal accounts, study questions, and a $32'' \times 11''$ timeline of events from 1831 through 1991.

Send: $5 (check or money order payable to the Smithsonian Institution)
Request: *Protest and Patriotism: A History of Dissent and Reform*
Send to: Office of Elementary and Secondary Education
Arts and Industries Building
1163/MRC 402
Smithsonian Institution
Washington, DC 20560

Milestone Events

This 50-page timeline of U.S. history provides students with a comprehensive overview of our country's progression from a struggling outpost of English settlers to the first nation to set foot on the moon. Photos, articles, and related activities, such as creating timelines of each student's life, are all coordinated with the seven major influential events that have been chosen as landmarks for our national journey of discovery.

Send: $4.50 (check or money order payable to Cobblestone Publishing)
Request: *Cobblestone Magazine: Famous Dates*
Send to: Cobblestone Publishing, Inc.
7 School St.
Peterborough, NH 03458

Let Freedom Ring

This extremely comprehensive curriculum package contains everything your need to create a one-, three-, or seven-day lesson plan exploring the important events of America's Civil Rights Movement. The kit includes a 38-minute documentary from acclaimed filmmaker Charles Guggenheim; *Free At Last*, a moving 108-page portrait of civil rights activists throughout history; and a 34-page teacher's guide with suggested activities and discussion topics.

Send: A letter of request from your school's principal
Request: *America's Civil Right Movement* teaching package
Send to: Teaching Tolerance
400 Washington Ave.
Montgomery, AL 36104

First Foothold

This detailed teacher's guide to Jamestown history lets you bring to life the turmoil, hardships, and eventual triumphs of the first settlers who attempted to establish communities on the American shores. Features a chronology of influential events, extensive background facts, insights into the practical aspects of daily life, and a wealth of authentic engraving prints, illustrations, supplemental activities, and bibliographical references.

Send: Your name and address on school stationery
Request: The Jamestown Settlement Museum Teacher Resource Packet
Send to: Education Department
Jamestown-Yorktown Foundation
P.O. Drawer JF
Williamsburg, VA 23185

Revolution!

Take your students on a journey to the heart of the American Revolution with this comprehensive teacher's guide. Kids can learn an authentic colonial game, sample the kinds of food rations revolutionary soldiers would have endured (actual recipes included!), discover the herbal preparations colonists used, learn folk songs from the period, and study the geography of our country's beginnings.

Send: Your name and address on school stationery
Request: Yorktown Victory Center Museum Teacher Resource Packet
Send to: Education Department
Jamestown-Yorktown Foundation
P.O. Drawer JF
Williamsburg, VA 23185

USA Map

Here's an inexpensive but extremely detailed view of the United States, complete with insets of Alaska, Hawaii, and all the U.S. territories. A giant $42'' \times 65''$ map of useful features including state lines, cities, rivers and other bodies of water, along with all national parks and monuments, fish and wildlife refuges, Indian reservations, and national forest lands, each named and outlined! An invaluable tool.

Send: $4.10 (check or money order payable to U.S. Geological Survey)
Request: Map 3A: Base Map of the United States
Send to: Branch of Distribution
U.S. Geological Survey
Box 25286, Federal Center
Denver, CO 80225

Symbol Savvy

To unlock all the valuable information a map has to offer you first have to crack the code. That means understanding the various symbols cartographers use to represent geological or man-made features. You can help make that task interesting and fun with a challenging game the entire class can play. Teach younger students or test older ones.

Send: $3 (check or money order payable to J. Berman's Orienteering Supply)
Request: The Map Symbol Relay Game
Send to: J. Berman's Orienteering Supply
P.O. Box 460
Sunderland, MA 01375-0460

State Stamps

Any child can recognize the ever-present red, white, and blue of our national banner but how many know what's depicted on the flag of their home state? Colorful expressions of each state's unique personality, flags make a great starting point for discussions on a range of topics from geography to Latin. These detailed stamps of each state's symbol help illustrate the cultural importance of flags.

Send: $3 (check or money order payable to the Jamestown Stamp Company)
Request: #Y-724: 50 U.S. State Flags
Send to: Jamestown Stamp Company
341 East Third St.
Jamestown, NY 14701-0019

Presidential Parade

Here's a neat visual aid for teaching about the presidents of the United States: colorful portraits of each of our 42 presidents, from George Washington through Bill Clinton. Use them as whole sheets or separate the seals and pass them around for closer inspection by students. An interesting way to connect 200 years of our history and give kids a new perspective on the presidency.

Send: $3.50 (check or money order payable to the Jamestown Stamp Company)
Request: #Y-723: 42 President Seals
Send to: Jamestown Stamp Company
341 East Third St.
Jamestown, NY 14701-0019

Orient Your Class!

Introduce them to the art and sport of orienteering. Orienteer training can intersect with a wide range of disciplines, since it requires such skills as interpretation of maps, mastering the compass, and observing and recording physical geography. Encourage an appreciation for teamwork, and have fun too! Get started with a beginner's guide to orienteering that covers map basics, compass parts, and a few technical tips.

Send: $1 (check or money order payable to J. Berman's Orienteering Supply)
Request: *Learn Orienteering*
Send to: J. Berman's Orienteering Supply
P.O. Box 460
Sunderland, MA 01375-0460

You Are Here

Integrate geography, reading, geometry, math skills, and navigational techniques with the help of this large $30'' \times 37''$ map designed by the map-making experts at the U.S. Geological Survey. It details various types of plot projections, including descriptions of how to use lines of longitude and latitude, map spacing, and map scale.

Send: $3.40 (check or money order payable to U.S. Geological Survey)
Request: Map I-1402: *The Properties and Uses of Selected Map Projections*
Send to: Branch of Distribution
U.S. Geological Survey
Box 25286, Federal Center
Denver, CO 80225

High Tech Geo

Put your students on-line with the National Geographic Kids Network, access interactive videodiscs that allow kids to create their own "textbooks," or discover the wonders of multimedia with CD-ROMs that contain encyclopedic information on a full range of subjects. To help you decide which program best suits your needs, this catalog provides a toll-free number where you can request items to preview for consideration.

Send: Your name and address
Or call: 1-800-368-2728
Request: The NGS Educational Technology Catalog
Send to: National Geographic Society
　　　　　Educational Services
　　　　　P.O. Box 98018
　　　　　Washington, DC 20090-8018

Geo Showdown

The final winner could walk away with a $25,000 college scholarship, but, win or lose, each participant is a little better for the effort. Not every student will win big, but all will become familiar with a globe, and *that's* the lasting effect of this wonderful program. You can get a registration kit for the National Geography Bee for free and decide whether you want your school to participate.

Send: A letter from the school you want to register (Only the principal may register a school to participate.)
Request: Registration kit for the National Geography Bee
Send to: National Geography Bee
　　　　　National Geographic Society
　　　　　1145 17th St. NW
　　　　　Washington, DC 20036-4688

Which Way Is North?

Prepare your preschool to primary grade students for a variety of academic pursuits with an enticing coloring-book introduction to the field of orienteering. The coloring book is designed to help four- to seven-year-olds understand a compass, map parts, elementary magnetism, and other concepts. Encourages reading and critical thinking skills.

Send: $5 (check or money order payable to J. Berman's Orienteering Supply)
Request: O ABC's: *The First Coloring Book About Orienteering*
Send to: J. Berman's Orienteering Supply
P.O. Box 460
Sunderland, MA 01375-0460

Follow Me!

The compass always points north, but what if you want to go west? Learning how to understand, set, and follow a compass employs a full range of skills that include reading, deduction, geometry, arithmetic, geography, and more. You can explore countless ways to challenge or test your students' navigational knowledge with the 100 different patterns included in this unique game.

Send: $3 (check or money order payable to J. Berman's Orienteering Supply)
Request: The Beginner's Compass Game
Send to: J. Berman's Orienteering Supply
P.O. Box 460
Sunderland, MA 01375-0460

Geo-Support

Sample support materials from the world's leading geo-graphic organization. The Geography Education Program costs, but you can get a free introductory packet with us-able items such as a 22″ × 35″ full-color poster depicting the five fundamental themes of geography and a sample issue of *Update*, which includes a listing of regional geo-alliance centers that coordinate additional activities.

Send: Your name and address
Request: Geography Education Program information folder
Send to: National Geographic Society
        Geography Education Program
        1145 17th St. NW
        Washington, DC 20036-4688

Teen Threads

You've seen how critical the right apparel can be to a stu-dent's sense of identity. This 43-page study of teens and clothing delves deep into the reasons for the importance of clothing to young people's identity. Lots of activities, discussion questions, essays, and a chance to participate in a Smithsonian research project.

Send: $5 (check or money order payable to the Smithso-nian Institution)
Request: *Image & Identity: Clothing and Adolescence in the 1990's*
Send to: Office of Elementary and Secondary Education
        Arts and Industries Building
        1163/MRC 402
        Smithsonian Institution
        Washington, DC 20560

Olympic Glory

There is something about the Olympic ideal that captivates and motivates us all. It's the stuff that children's dreams are made of, and the quest for Olympic glory begins early for today's competitors. You can use your students' inherent attraction to the thrill of sporting competition as a springboard to a variety of subjects. Touch on ancient Greek history and culture, social studies, current events, geography, the economics of hosting the games, or athletic endeavor in general; a study of the Olympic Games can lead through many worlds.

Here's the definitive guide to the Olympics, 38 full-color pages packed with every statistic, detail, custom, and historical reference you could want. Who wrote the Olympic hymn? How many times have the Olympic games been held in the United States? How many gold medals did the U.S. win in the 1896 games? Where will the Olympic games be held in the year 2000? It's all in here, from an explanation of the various governing bodies and international committees to what an Olympic athlete eats to stay fit. Also included is information about the worldwide Paralympic Games (held every four years in conjunction with the Olympics), plus bibliographical resources to check for further research.

Send: Your name and address
Request: The publication *Inside of the Olympic Movement*
Send to: The United States Olympic Committee
        One Olympic Plaza
        Colorado Springs, CO 80909-5760

Big Themes

This educator guide uses seven popular books as the foundation for a thematic program based on the broad topic of multiculturalism. Emphasizing the whole-language approach, a detailed activities flow chart helps you target specific skills within the overall project, from introductory exercises to follow-up discussion questions. Includes 25 pages of experiments, art and craft ideas, creative writing assignments, even a letter to send home for parents.

Send: Your name and address on school stationery
Request: *Big Themes Unit Management Guide to Multiculturalism*
Send to: Sundance Publishing
234 Taylor St.
Littleton, MA 01460

The Story of Soap

What was the first civilization to use soap? Which countries eventually led the way to the commercial production of soap? Where do the ingredients for soap come from? Is there a difference between soap and detergent? The answers to these and hundreds of other questions can be found in this informative 34-page publication filled with soap facts, from the chemistry of soap to its surprising history.

Send: Your name and address
Request: The publication *Soaps and Detergents*
Send to: The Soap and Detergent Association
475 Park Ave. South
New York, NY 10016

Human Rights

Are there universal rights that should be afforded to all peoples of the earth? What would your students say those rights were? Are those rights and privileges always upheld in every country around the world? This 16-page booklet delineates the International Bill of Rights as set forth and defended by the United Nations. Its 30 articles of declaration touch on all aspects of the human condition.

Send: Your name and address on school stationery
Request: A copy of the *Universal Declaration of Human Rights*
Send to: Public Inquiries Unit
Public Services Section
Department of Public Information
The United Nations
New York, NY 10017

Teaching Tolerance

Cultural, racial, economic, and political diversity is the tradition of American society. The goal of *Teaching Tolerance* is to encourage a nationwide atmosphere of acceptance for, even exhilaration in, the differences among us. The beautifully produced, 65-page, full-color magazine provides ongoing support to thousands of educators around the country interested in nurturing a greater spirit of community among their students. Ask for a free sample copy.

Send: Your name and address on school stationery
Request: A copy of *Teaching Tolerance* magazine
Send to: Teaching Tolerance
400 Washington Ave.
Montgomery, AL 36104

Where can you get the most detailed, up-to-date maps of any state, discover the kinds of little-known facts and fun tidbits of information you can only learn from the people who actually live in a place, tie together the subjects of geography, culture, history, ecology, earth science, sociology, and so much more, all for only the effort of placing a simple toll-free phone call? Right here. Each of the 50 states in America puts together an extensive collection of enticing materials that portray their home as the people who live there see it. These extremely detailed, artistic, visually impressive publications cover every aspect of a state from key government officials and the legislative structure to the official state bird or flower. State history, influential residents, physical geography, climate, population, economic statistics, stunning nature photographs, plus insight into popular social events, celebrations, and other cultural activities make these packets of information a gold mine of ideas for innovative teachers.

Almost every state has a toll-free number to call and request a free tourism package, with the exceptions of Alaska, Florida, and New Hampshire. It's still possible to call these states (just not toll free) or write them.

Alabama
Alabama Bureau of Tourism
401 Adams Ave.
P.O. Box 4309
Montgomery, AL 36104
1-800-ALABAMA (1-800-252-2262)

Alaska
Alaska Division of Tourism
P.O. Box 110801
Juneau, AK 99811-0801
1-900-465-2010

Arizona
Arizona Office of Tourism
1100 West Washington
Phoenix, AZ 85007
1-800-842-8257

Arkansas
Arkansas Department of
Parks & Tourism
One Capitol Mall
Little Rock, AR 72201
1-800-NATURAL (1-800-628-
8725)

California
California Office of Tourism
801 K St.
Sacramento, CA 95814
1-800-862-2543

Colorado
Colorado Tourism Board
1625 Broadway, Suite 1700
Denver, CO 80202
1-800-433-2656

Connecticut
Tourism Division
865 Brook St.
Rocky Hill, CT 06067-3405
1-800-282-6863

Delaware
Delaware Development
Office
99 Kings Hwy.
P.O. Box 1401
Dover, DE 19903
1-800-441-8846

District of Columbia
Washington Convention &
Visitor Association
P.O. Box 27489
Washington, DC 20038-7489
1-800-422-8644

Florida
Bureau of Visitor Services
107 West Gaines St.,
Room 501D
Tallahassee, FL 32399-2000
1-904-487-1462
(Besides maps, guides, and
other info, this package also
includes a listing of all the
800 numbers for tourist information from each region
or locale.)

Georgia
Convention & Visitors
Bureau
233 Peachtree St.,
Suite 2000
Atlanta, GA 30303
1-800-VISIT-GA (1-800-847-
4842)

Hawaii
Hawaii Visitors Bureau
2270 Kalakaua Ave.
Honolulu, HI 96815
1-800-VISIT-HI (1-800-847-
4844)

Idaho
Idaho Travel Council
State House Mall
700 West State St.
Boise, ID 83720-2700
1-800-635-7820

Illinois
Illinois Tourist Information
Center
P.O. Box 7905
Mt. Prospect, IL 60056-7905
1-800-223-0121

Indiana
Tourism Development
1 North Capitol, Suite 700
Indianapolis, IN 46204
1-800-289-6646

Iowa
Division of Tourism
200 East Grand Ave.
Des Moines, IA 50309
1-800-345-4692

Kansas
Kansas Travel & Tourism Information
700 SW Harrison, Suite 1300
Topeka, KS 66603
1-800-252-6727

Kentucky
Tourism Cabinet
Capitol Plaza Tower
500 Mero St., Suite 22
Frankfort, KY 40601
1-800-225-TRIP (1-800-225-
8747)

Louisiana
Louisiana Office of Tourism
P.O. Box 94291
Baton Rouge, LA 70804-
9291
1-800-334-8626

Maine
Publicity Bureau
P.O. Box 2300
Hallowell, ME 04347
1-800-533-9595

Maryland
Office of Tourism
217 East Redwood St.
Baltimore, MD 21202
1-800-543-1036

Massachusetts
Massachusetts Travel &
Tourism
100 Cambridge St.,
13th Floor
Boston, MA 02202
1-800-447-6277

Michigan
Michigan Travel Bureau
P.O. Box 3393
Livonia, MI 48151-3393
1-800-543-2937

Minnesota
Minnesota Office of Tourism
100 Metro Square Building
121 Seventh Pl. East
St. Paul, MN 55101
1-800-657-3700

Mississippi
Division of Tourism
P.O. Box 1705
Ocean Springs, MS 39566-
1705
1-800-927-6378

Missouri
Visitors Bureau
City Center Square
1100 Main, Suite 2550
Kansas City, MO 64105
1-800-767-7700

Montana
Travel Promotion
1424 Ninth Ave.
Helena, MT 59620
1-800-VISIT-MT (1-800-847-
4868)

Nebraska
Travel & Tourism Division
301 Centennial Mall South
P.O. Box 94666
Lincoln, NE 68509
1-800-228-4307

Nevada
Commission of Tourism
5151 South Carson St.
Carson City, NV 89710
1-800-638-2328

New Hampshire
Vacation Travel
P.O. Box 1856
Concord, NH 03302
1-603-271-2348

New Jersey
Division of Tourism
P.O. Box CN 826
Trenton, NJ 08625
1-800-537-7397

New Mexico
Department of Tourism
Lamy Building
491 Old Santa Fe Trail
Santa Fe, NM 87503
1-800-545-2040

New York
Division of Tourism
One Commerce Plaza
Albany, NY 12245
1-800-225-5697

North Carolina
Travel & Tourism Division
430 North Salisbury St.
Raleigh, NC 27603
1-800-VISIT-NC (1-800-847-
4862)

North Dakota
Travel Department
Liberty Memorial Building
604 East Blvd.
Bismark, ND 58505
1-800-435-5063

Ohio
Office of Travel & Tourism
77 South High St.,
29th Floor
Columbus, OH 43266
1-800-BUCKEYE (1-800-282-
5393)

Oklahoma
Tourism & Recreation
Department
P.O. Box 60789
Oklahoma City, OK 73146
1-800-652-6552

Oregon
Tourism Division
775 Summer St. NE
Salem, OR 97310
1-800-547-7842

Pennsylvania
Bureau of Travel
Development
453 Forum Building
Harrisburg, PA 17120
1-800-VISIT-PA (1-800-847-
4872)

Rhode Island
Tourist Promotion Division
Seven Jackson Walkway
Providence, RI 02903
1-800-556-2484

South Carolina
Division of Tourism
1205 Pendleton St.
Columbia, SC 29201
1-800-346-3634

South Dakota
Department of Tourism
711 East Wells Ave.
Pierre, SD 57501-3369
1-800-732-5682

Tennessee
Tourist Development
P.O. Box 23170
Nashville, TN 37202
1-800-843-9861

Texas
Tourism Division
P.O. Box 12728
Austin, TX 78711-2728
1-800-888-8839

Utah
Travel Council
Council Hall, Capitol Hill
Salt Lake City, UT 84114
1-800-UTAH-FUN (1-800-882-4386)

Vermont
Travel Division
134 State St.
Montpelier, VT 05602
1-800-837-6668

Virginia
Division of Tourism
1021 East Cary
Richmond, VA 23219
1-800-VISIT-VA (1-800-847-4882)

Washington
Tourism Development
Division
P.O. Box 42500
Olympia, WA 98504-2500
1-800-544-1800

West Virginia
Division of Tourism & Parks
1900 Kanawha Blvd.
Building 6, Room B564
Charleston, WV 25305-0317
1-800-225-5982

Wisconsin
Tourism
P.O. Box 7606
Madison, WI 53707
1-800-432-8747

Wyoming
Travel Commission
1-25 at College Dr.
Cheyenne, WY 82002
1-800-225-5996

There's no better way to get to know the people of a country than to talk with them personally. Although global field trips are not realistically possible, you can still take your class into the heart of any culture through the generous packets of information distributed by the embassies, consulates, and tourist bureaus of each nation. Each country prepares its own—often surprisingly sophisticated and extensive—collection of books, magazines, videos, and other instructional aids. These publications suggest countless ways to teach about a country's geography, history, culture, language, political system, climate, economy, or other characteristics, and since they come from the region being studied they often provide rare insights into a nation's true essence.

In this listing, you'll find both the consulate information and any tourist board telephone numbers that may apply to a given country. (Some have both, others do not.) The separate offices often produce quite different items. For example, the tourism office might have gorgeous photos or maps but the consulate can offer in-depth books about the country's history or political structure. Because of space limitations, we could not include every country. Instead, we've tried to include popularly studied countries and countries from every continent.

Send: Your name and address on school stationery (Identifying yourself as a professional elicits the best publications.)
Request: Promotional brochures, travel materials, or general information, whatever suits your needs (The more specific you are the better you'll be served.)
Send to: The country of interest

Argentina
Consulate General of
Argentina
Cultural Office
12 West 56th St.
New York, NY 10019
212-603-0400

Australia
Australian Information
Service
630 Fifth Ave., Suite 420
New York, NY 10111
212-408-8400

Austria
Consulate General of
Austria
950 Third Ave., 20th Floor
New York, NY 10022
212-737-6400
National Tourist Office: 310-
477-3332

Bahamas
Consulate General of the
Bahamas
231 East 46th St.
New York, NY 10017
212-421-6420
Tourist Office: 212-758-2777

Bangladesh
Consulate General of
Bangladesh
211 East 43rd St., Suite 502
New York, NY 10017
212-599-6767

Barbados
Consulate General of
Barbados
800 Second Ave., 18th Floor
New York, NY 10017
212-867-8431
Board of Tourism: 212-986-
6516

Belarus
Mission of the Republic of
Belarus
136 East 67th St.
New York, NY 10021
212-535-3420

Belgium
Consulate General of
Belgium
1330 Avenue of the Ameri-
cas, 26th Floor
New York, NY 10019
212-586-5110
Tourist Office: 212-758-8130

Belize
Embassy of Belize
2535 Massachusetts Ave.
NW
Washington, DC 20008
202-332-9636

Bolivia
Consulate General of
Bolivia
211 East 43rd St., Room 702
New York, NY 10017
212-687-0530

Botswana
Embassy of Botswana
3400 International Dr. NW,
Suite 7M
Washington, DC 20008
202-244-4990

Brazil
Consulate General of Brazil
630 Fifth Ave., Room 2720
New York, NY 10111
212-757-3080

British Tourist Office
40 West 57th St.
New York, NY 10019
212-581-4700

Bulgaria
Embassy of the Republic of
Bulgaria
Public Relations
1621 22nd St. NW
Washington, DC 20008
202-387-7969

Burkina Faso
Embassy of Burkina Faso
2340 Massachusetts Ave.
NW
Washington, DC 20008
202-332-5577

Cameroon
Embassy of the Republic of
Cameroon
2349 Massachusetts Ave.
NW
Washington, DC 20008
202-265-8790

Canada
Canadian Consul Library Information Center
1251 Avenue of the
Americas
New York, NY 10020-1175
212-596-1600

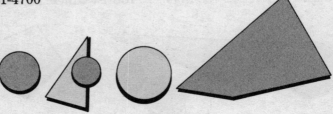

Cape Verde
Consulate General of Cape
Verde
535 Boylston St., 2nd Floor
Boston, MA 02116
617-353-0014

Chile
Consulate General of Chile
866 United Nations Plaza,
Room 302
New York, NY 10017
212-980-3366

China
Consulate General of the
People's Republic of China
Cultural Office
520 Twelfth St.
New York, NY 10036
212-330-7425
Tourist Board: 212-760-9700

Colombia
Columbian Consulate
1825 Connecticut Ave. NW
Washington, DC 20009
202-332-7476

Costa Rica
Consulate General of Costa
Rica
80 Wall St.
New York, NY 10005
212-425-2620

Cyprus
Consulate General of
Cyprus
13 East 40th St.
New York, NY 10016
212-686-6016

Denmark
Royal Danish Consulate
General
885 Second Ave., 18th Floor
New York, NY 10017-2201
212-223-4545
Tourist Board: 212-949-2333

Ecuador
Embassy of Ecuador
2535 15th St. NW
Washington, DC 20009
202-234-7200

Estonia
Mission of the Republic of
Estonia
630 Fifth Ave., Suite 2415
New York, NY 10111
212-247-0499

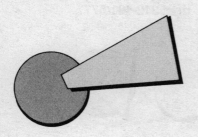

Ethiopia
Ethiopian Consulate
866 United Nations Plaza,
Room 560
New York, NY 10017
212-421-1830

Fiji
Consulate General of Fiji
One United Nations Plaza,
26th Floor
New York, NY 10017
212-355-7316

Finland
Consulate General of
Finland
866 United Nations Plaza,
Suite 250
New York, NY 10017
212-750-4400
Tourist Board: 212-949-2333

France
French Cultural Service
972 Fifth Ave.
New York, NY 10021
212-439-1400
Government Tourist Office:
212-838-7800

Gabon
Embassy of the Republic of
Gabon
2034 20th St. NW
Washington, DC 20009
202-797-1000

Georgia
Embassy of the Republic of
Georgia
1511 K St., Suite 424
Washington, DC 20005
202-393-6060

Germany
German Information Center
950 Third Ave., 24th Floor
New York, NY 10022
212-888-9840
National Tourist Office: 212-
661-7200

Greece
Greek Press and Informa-
tion Office
601 Fifth Ave., 3rd Floor
New York, NY 10017
212-751-8788
National Tourist Organization: 212-421-5777

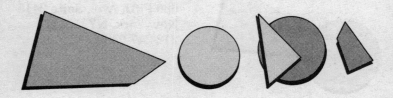

Guatemala
Consulate General of
Guatemala
299 Alhambra Circle,
Suite 510
Coral Gables, FL 33134
1-800-742-4529

Honduras
Embassy of Honduras
3007 Tilden St. NW
POD-4M
Washington, DC 20008
202-966-9750
Tourist Bureau: 213-682-3377

**Hong Kong Tourist
Association**
590 Fifth Ave.
New York, NY 10036
212-869-5008

Hungary
Consulate General of the
Republic of Hungary
223 East 52nd St.
New York, NY 10022
212-752-0661

Iceland
Consulate General of
Iceland
370 Lexington Ave., 5th
Floor
New York, NY 10017
212-686-4100

India
Consulate General of India
Information Section
3 East 64th St.
New York, NY 10021
212-879-8048
Tourist Office: 212-586-4901

Indonesia
Consulate General of
Indonesia
5 East 68th St.
New York, NY 10021
212-879-0600
Tourist Office: 213-387-2078

Ireland
Consulate General of
Ireland
345 Park Ave. at 51st, 17th
Floor
New York, NY 10037
212-319-2555
Tourist Board: 212-418-0800

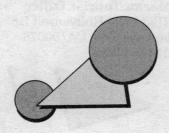

Israel

Consulate General of Israel
Information Office
800 Second Ave., 13th Floor
New York, NY 10017
212-499-5300
Government Tourist Office:
212-560-0621

Italy

Italian Government Travel
Office
630 Fifth Ave., Suite 1565
New York, NY 10111
212-245-4822
Tourist Office: 212-245-4961

Jamaica

Consulate General of
Jamaica
Information Service
767 Third Ave.
New York, NY 10017
212-935-9000
Tourist Board: 212-688-7650

Japan

Consulate General of Japan
Japan Information Center
299 Park Ave., 16th Floor
New York, NY 10171-0025
212-371-8222
National Tourist Office: 415-
989-7140

Kenya

Embassy of Kenya
2249 R St. NW
Washington, DC 20008
202-387-6101
Tourist Office: 212-486-1300

Kuwait

Consulate General of
Kuwait
321 East 44th St.
New York, NY 10017
212-973-4318

Laos

Embassy of the Lao
People's Democratic
Republic
2222 S St. NW
Washington, DC 20008
202-332-6416

Luxembourg

Luxembourg National
Tourist Office
17 Beekman Pl.
New York, NY 10022
212-935-8888

Macau Tourist Office

3133 Lake Hollywood Dr.
Los Angeles, CA 90078
213-851-3402

Madagascar
Embassy of Madagascar
Cultural Attache
2374 Massachusetts Ave.
NW
Washington, DC 20008
202-265-5525

Malaysian Tourist Centre
818 West 7th St.
Los Angeles, CA 90017
213-689-9702

Mexico
Consulate General of
Mexico
8 East 41st St.
New York, NY 10017
212-689-0456

Mongolia
Embassy of Mongolia
2833 M St. NW
Washington, DC 20007
202-298-7137

Morocco
Consulate General of
Morocco
20 East 46th St., Suite 1202
New York, NY 10017
212-557-2520

Mozambique
Consulate General of
Mozambique
1990 M St. NW, Suite 570
Washington, DC 20036
202-293-7146

Namibia
Mission of the Republic of
Namibia
135 East 36th St.
New York, NY 10016
212-685-2003

Nepal
Royal Nepalese Embassy
2131 Leroy Pl. NW
Washington, DC 20008
202-667-4550

Netherlands
Consulate General of the
Netherlands
One Rockefeller Plaza, 11th
Floor
New York, NY 10020
212-246-1429
Board of Tourism: 312-819-
0300

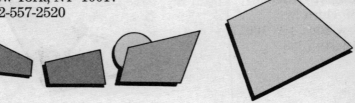

New Zealand
New Zealand Tourism
Board
501 Santa Monica Blvd.,
Suite 300
Santa Monica, CA 90401
1-800-388-5494

Nicaragua
Mission of Nicaragua
Information Officer
820 Second Ave., 8th Floor
New York, NY 10017
212-490-7997

Nigeria
Nigerian Information
Services
828 Second Ave.
New York, NY 10017
212-808-0301

Norway
Norwegian Information
Service
825 Third Ave., 38th Floor
New York, NY 10022
212-421-7333

**Norway Scandinavia
Tourist Offices**
655 Third Ave.
New York, NY 10017
212-949-2333

Oman
Mission of Oman
866 United Nations Plaza,
Suite 540
New York, NY 10017
212-355-3505

Pakistan
Mission of Pakistan
Press Attache
8 East 65th St.
New York, NY 10021
212-879-8600

Panama
Consulate General of
Panama
1212 Avenue of the Americas, 10th Floor
New York, NY 10036
212-840-2450

Paraguay
Consulate General of
Paraguay
675 Third Ave., Suite 1604
New York, NY 10017
212-682-9441

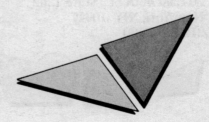

Philippines
Consulate General of the
Philippines
Cultural Office
556 Fifth Ave.
New York, NY 10036
212-764-1330
Department of Tourism:
213-487-4525

Poland
Consulate General of the
Republic of Poland
233 Madison Ave.
New York, NY 10016
212-889-8360

Portugal
Embassy of Portugal
Cultural Attache
2125 Kalorama Rd. NW
Washington, DC 20008
202-328-8610
Tourism Office: 212-354-4403

Puerto Rico
Puerto Rican Tourism Office
1290 Avenue of the
Americas
New York, NY 10104
212-599-6262

Quebec Tourism
17 West 50th St.
New York, NY 10020
1-800-363-7777

Romania
Romanian Cultural Centre
200 East 38th St.
New York, NY 10016
212-687-0181
National Tourist Offices:
212-697-6971

Russian Federation
Mission of the Russian
Federation
Public Relations Office
136 East 67th St.
New York, NY 10021
212-861-4900
Travel Information Office:
212-757-3884

Rwanda
Consulate General of
Rwanda
336 East 45th St., 3rd Floor
New York, NY 10017
212-808-9330

Samoa
Independent State of
Western Samoa
820 Second Ave., Suite 800D
New York, NY 10017
212-599-6196

Saudi Arabia
Royal Saudi Arabian
Embassy
Information Office
601 New Hampshire Ave.
NW
Washington, DC 20037
202-342-3800

Senegal
Mission of the Republic of
Senegal
238 East 68th St.
New York, NY 10021
212-517-9030

Seychelles
Mission of the Republic of
Seychelles
820 Second Ave., Suite 900F
New York, NY 10017
212-687-9766

Sierra Leone
Mission of Sierra Leone
245 East 49th St.
New York, NY 10017
212-688-4985

Singapore
Mission of Singapore
231 East 51st St.
New York, NY 10022
212-826-0840
Tourist Board: 212-302-4861

South Africa
Consulate General of South
Africa
333 East 38th St., 9th Floor
New York, NY 10016
212-213-4880
Tourism Board: 212-838-8841

Spain
Embassy of Spain
Information Office
2375 Pennsylvania Ave. NW
Washington, DC 20037
202-452-0100
National Tourism Office:
212-759-8822

Sri Lanka
Embassy of Sri Lanka
Information Service
2148 Wyoming Ave. NW
Washington, DC 20008
202-483-4025

Sudan
Embassy of the Republic of
the Sudan
2210 Massachusetts Ave.
NW
Washington, DC 20008
202-338-8565

Suriname
Consulate General of the
Republic of Suriname
7235 NW 19th St., Suite A
Miami, FL 33126
305-593-2163

Swaziland
Embassy of the Kingdom of
Swaziland
3400 International Dr.,
Suite 3M
Washington, DC 20008
202-362-6683

Sweden
Swedish Information
Service
885 Second Ave., 45th Floor
New York, NY 10017
212-751-5900
Tourist Board: 212-949-2333

Switzerland
Consulate General of
Switzerland
665 Fifth Ave., 8th Floor
New York, NY 10022
212-758-2560
National Tourist Board: 212-
757-5944

Tanzania
Embassy of the United Re-
public of Tanzania
2139 R St. NW
Washington, DC 20008
202-939-6125

Thailand
Tourism Authority of
Thailand
5 World Trade Center, Suite
3443
New York, NY 10048
212-432-0433
Tourism Authority: 213-382-
2353

Trinidad and Tobago
Consulate of Trinidad and
Tobago
733 Third Ave., Suite 1716
New York, NY 10017-3204
212-682-7272
Tourist Board: 212-719-0540

Turkey
Turkish Tourism and Information Office
821 United Nations Plaza,
4th floor
New York, NY 10017
212-687-2194

Ukraine
Mission of Ukraine
Public Relations Office
136 East 67th St.
New York, NY 10021
212-535-3418

United Kingdom
British Information Services
845 Third Ave.
New York, NY 10022
212-752-5747
Tourism Offices: 1-800-462-2748

Uruguay
Consulate General of
Uruguay
747 Third Ave., 21st Floor
New York, NY 10017
212-753-8191

Venezuela
Consulate General of
Venezuela
7 East 51st St.
New York, NY 10022
212-826-1660
Tourist Bureau: 212-766-2288

Virgin Islands Tourism Office
1270 Avenue of the
Americas
New York, NY 10021
212-332-2222

Zambia
Zambia National Tourist
Board
237 East 52nd St.
New York, NY 10022
212-758-1110

Zimbabwe
Embassy of Zimbabwe
1608 New Hampshire Ave.
NW
Washington, DC 20009
202-332-7100

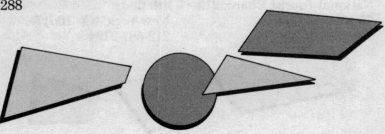

Language Arts

The Bard

Enhance those often obscure Shakespearean references with some visual insight into the age in which they originated. Students can examine styles of dress, see historic sites, and get a real feel for the time. This set of 30 quality art prints (5″ × 8″ size) adds depth to literature studies.

Send: $3.50 (check or money order payable to The University Prints)
Request: *Shakespeare's World*
Send to: The University Prints
21 East St.
P.O. Box 485
Winchester, MA 01890

Space ABCs

This informative coloring book was designed by NASA to help educators introduce students in the primary grades to space-oriented language, equipment, and concepts. Take kids from Astronaut through Zero-gravity with the full-page reproducibles of each letter and its space-related drawing. Younger kids can simply study letters and color in the pictures; older students will enjoy the captions with more advanced details about each subject.

Send: Your name and address on school stationery
Request: *My ABC Space Book* coloring book
Send to: See "NASA Addresses," pages 146-147

A Classic Revisited

Take advantage of some modern name recognition to spark your students' interest in classic literature. The child-friendly coloring book format draws young readers into the world of the original Hans Christian Andersen tale *The Little Mermaid*, where they can bring color to the beautiful W. Heath Robinson illustrations while practicing their reading skills. Touch on history, social studies, reading, and language arts, all with a coloring book!

Send: $4.95 (check or money order payable to Bellerophon Books; CA residents add appropriate sales tax)
Request: #039-3: *The Little Mermaid*
Send to: Bellerophon Books
        36 Anacapa St.
        Santa Barbara, CA 93101

The Process

After experiencing the advantages of whole-language reading programs, students in grades three through eight often benefit from the use of those same techniques to learn creative writing skills. This 12-page guide to narrative prose provides ideas and activities that can help kids see that writing is a *process* of collecting and organizing ideas. By dissecting specific genres and authors' tricks of the trade, students learn to construct their own original works.

Send: Your name and address on school stationery
Request: Genre Writing Program sampler: *Writing in Narrative Form*
Send to: Sundance Publishing
        234 Taylor St.
        Littleton, MA 01460

Little Red Readers

These little red books are designed to give beginning readers the kind of recognizable progressions, easy-to-master vocabulary, and familiar subject matter that will encourage confident advancement through increasingly complex sentence and word structure. Colorful illustrations complement each eight-page text and provide clues to new words added to the basic pattern.

Send: Your name and address on school stationery
Request: A sample *Little Red Reader* set
Send to: Sundance Publishing
234 Taylor St.
Littleton, MA 01460

The "Muse" in Museum

Though you may not have access to a collection like the Smithsonian's, you can still use local or regional museums to inspire your students' creativity in new and original ways. This well-crafted 65-page guide focuses on the process of writing, collecting, assimilating, and reshaping information through the filter of our individual perceptions. Contains detailed activities, course objectives, and lesson plans.

Send: $5 (check or money order payable to the Smithsonian Institution)
Request: *Collecting Their Thoughts: Using Museums as Resources for Student Writing*
Send to: Office of Elementary and Secondary Education
Arts and Industries Building
1163/MRC 402
Smithsonian Institution
Washington, DC 20560

Literacy Club

Based on seven years of implementation at a school that services nearly 700 language-minority students, the Literacy Club offers a cross-cultural, age-integrated approach to mainstreaming bilingual kids. By pairing sixth graders with first-grade pupils, the club helps enhance not only literacy acquisition but social skills as well.

Send: $3.50 (check or money order payable to the NCBE)
Request: Program Information Guide #13: *The Literacy Club: A Cross-Age Tutoring/Paired Reading Project*
Send to: The National Clearinghouse for
Bilingual Education
1118 22nd St. NW
Washington, DC 20037

Learning Links

As decades of studies on teaching techniques have dramatically illustrated, literature-based reading, writing, and language arts instruction is an effective, engaging, student-friendly means to nurture a lifelong love of prose in all its forms. Learning Links supports that ideal with an 85-page catalog of interrelated books and activity guides that link language to every other element in a curriculum. Sample pages from selected materials are available at no cost.

Send: Your name and address
Or call: 1-800-724-2616
Request: The latest Learning Links catalog and sample pages from materials related to your grade or subject needs
Send to: Learning Links, Inc.
2300 Marcus Ave.
New Hyde Park, NY 11042

Hearing the Call of the Wild

Using *The Call of the Wild* as the basis for dozens of language arts activities, this active reading guide from the *Novel Ideas* series presents interactive quizzes and lesson plans for kids in grades seven through 12. The idea is to help kids see literature as an encounter with characters that can become lifelong friends. The 32-page guide features interpretations of plot, character, narrative, setting, and sections for students' personal responses.

Send: Your name and address on school stationery
Request: A sample copy of *Novel Ideas Plus: Active Reading Guide—The Call of the Wild*
Send to: Sundance Publishing
       234 Taylor St.
       Littleton, MA 01460

Language Link

Specializing in computer software programs for language arts, Teacher Support Software provides a line of innovative tools to involve your class in a variety of creative writing projects. You can design and print books, flash cards, worksheets, vocabulary lists, and more. Students can develop essential skills through whole-language or basal approaches. Ask for the free catalog and demo disk.

Send: Your name and address
Or call: 1-800-228-2871
Request: The latest Teacher Support Software catalogs and demo disk
Send to: Teacher Support Software
       1035 NW 57th St.
       Gainesville, FL 32605-4486

Literature Specialists

Don't waste valuable budget dollars on books children won't want to read. You can get expert advice from professional children's literature specialists who can help you create an engaging and effective whole-language reading list. The Association of Booksellers for Children will send you a list of local members you can consult about popular titles, developmentally appropriate stories, and any special subject needs you have.

Send: Your name and address
Request: The locator list of children's literature specialists in your area
Send to: Association of Booksellers for Children
4412 Chowen Ave. South, #303
Minneapolis, MN 55410

First Person

It's history, language study, and adventure of the highest order, all in a beautifully illustrated coloring book guaranteed to capture students' imagination. Let them experience the historic voyage of Christopher Columbus as he described it in his own words. The easy-to-read large type tells the story in both English and Spanish! A great starting point for a variety of studies.

Send: $4.95 (check or money order payable to Bellerophon Books; CA residents add appropriate sales tax)
Request: #156-X: *Christopher Columbus*
Send to: Bellerophon Books
36 Anacapa St.
Santa Barbara, CA 93101

Dramatic Ideas

Long known for its ability to send the heads of even the most attentive students reeling with obscure references and arcane usage of the English language, the much-studied tragedy of *Macbeth* unfolds with renewed excitement in this unique "active reading guide." Designed for students in grades seven through 12, it includes 32 pages of interactive language exercises, vocabulary lists, group projects, study questions, and even SAT test tips.

Send: Your name and address on school stationery
Request: *Dramatic Ideas Active Reading Guide: Macbeth*
Send to: Sundance Publishing
234 Taylor St.
Littleton, MA 01460

Opposing Viewpoints

Debate is what the *Opposing Viewpoints* publications are designed to encourage. Each 136-page position paper effectively presents both sides of a controversial social issue, with opinions supplied by the most prominent, respected figures in that field. Hundreds of individual viewpoint booklets are only $3.50 to teachers and librarians. To decide which would best fit your classroom situation, start with the 68-page Greenhaven Press catalog.

Send: Your name and address
Or call: 1-800-231-5163
Request: The latest edition of the Greenhaven Press catalog
Send to: Greenhaven Press
P.O. Box 289009
San Diego, CA 92198-9009

Cricket

This monthly magazine has been a staple children's language arts periodical for more than 20 years. An updated format now boasts larger pages, full-color illustrations, photos, and a recurring cartoon strip. The stories are often excerpts of popular works, done especially for *Cricket*. Characters, places, and issues of interest to kids ages nine to 14. Order a copy and check it out.

Send: $4 (check or money order payable to *Cricket* magazine)
Request: A copy of the latest issue of *Cricket*
Send to: Cricket
      315 Fifth Ave.
      P.O. Box 300
      Peru, IL 61354-0300

Spider

Spider is designed for kids ages six to nine, who are just beginning to read confidently on their own. The award-winning stories are challenging but developmentally appropriate. Charming illustrations from respected artists depict the work of popular authors. A wealth of enticing language arts projects, hidden word puzzles, poems, games, and a four-page activity supplement come with each issue. Order a copy of the most recent issue.

Send: $4 (check or money order payable to *Spider* magazine)
Request: A copy of the latest issue of *Spider*
Send to: Spider
      315 Fifth Ave.
      P.O. Box 300
      Peru, IL 61354-0300

Reading Large

Big books let the whole class see and enjoy a story's words and pictures. This useful planning calendar showcases big books. For each month of the school year it focuses on a theme (such as beginnings, friendship, community, peace, and family) and a colorful giant-format book that illustrates the month's topic. A full-page universal calendar helps you organize lessons.

Send: Your name and address on school stationery
Request: The *Multicultural Big Book Calendar*
Send to: Sundance Publishing
234 Taylor St.
Littleton, MA 01460

Ladybug

Each monthly issue of *Ladybug* (for kids ages two to six) is a collection of mini storybooks written and illustrated by some of the most popular children's literature artists from around the world. Every volume features a special song, poems, animal adventures, a removable four-page insert with projects to construct and color, plus a supplementary advice section with tips for involving parents in skill-builder activities at home. You can order an individual copy to examine *Ladybug* for yourself.

Send: $4 (check or money order payable to *Ladybug* Magazine)
Request: A copy of the latest issue of *Ladybug*
Send to: Ladybug
315 Fifth Ave.
P.O. Box 300
Peru, IL 61354-0300

Generations

Great literature helps kids understand the universality of their personal emotional struggles. This eight-page guide to the novel *The Joy Luck Club* uses the intertwined life stories of two generations of Chinese women to inspire creative writing, language, and reading activities. A final 50-item test on the material includes vocabulary lists and sections of true/false, fill-in-the-blanks, and matching exercises, as well as essay questions.

Send: Your name and address on school stationery
Request: *Novel Ideas Teacher Reference Guide: The Joy Luck Club*
Send to: Sundance Publishing
234 Taylor St.
Littleton, MA 01460

Literature List

If you're looking for some new materials that can help your students sharpen their language and reading skills while nurturing an appreciation of the world's peoples and cultures, this educator reference list can help. It catalogs hundreds of individual titles of popular children's books. Twelve pages, categorized according to grade levels from K through 12, indicate the ethnic, racial, or cultural focus of each book and where the book can be found.

Send: Your name and address on school stationery
Request: *Sundance Multicultural Literature Listing*
Send to: Sundance Publishing
234 Taylor St.
Littleton, MA 01460

Environment & Conservation

This Island Earth

Earth Island Institute was the driving force behind the international boycott responsible for altering tuna fishing practices around the globe. The Institute and the International Marine Mammal Project have also been closely involved with the creators of the popular children's film *Free Willy*, and they've now collaborated with Warner Bros. Pictures and Bumble Bee Tuna to produce a collection of educational materials. Capitalizing on the immense response to the film and children's widespread interest in the whale who played Willy, the package of publications is designed to bring students all over the country a deeper awareness of marine animals and illustrate the delicate balance of life in the ocean. The kit includes a large full-color poster depicting the relative sizes, shapes, and markings of various species of whales and dolphins; a complete teacher's guide with background information and reproducibles; and directions for activities that incorporate facts about marine life with mathematics exercises, reading skills, and language arts. You also get 60 marine animal picture "milk cap" game pieces.

Send: $3 for shipping costs
Request: The *Life in the Sea* Discovery Kit
Send to: Earth Island Institute
300 Broadway, Suite 28
San Francisco, CA 94133

Documentary Drama

The Video Project is a nonprofit organization dedicated to presenting the world's most impressive documentary programs. This 65-page catalog provides access to hundreds of award-winning films, all concerned with the health of planet earth. Video purchase or rentals with reduced fees for low-income groups.

Send: Your name and address
Or call: 1-800-4-PLANET
Request: The latest Video Project documentary catalog
Send to: The Video Project
Films and Videos for a Safe & Sustainable World
5332 College Ave., Suite 101
Oakland, CA 94618

Pollution Problems

What is an aquifer and how might various forms of pollution affect its purity? Can you track pollution in a water supply back to its source? Students work out solutions to these problems and others with the experiments in this educator's guide. They'll clean fouled water, construct an aquifer, and play pollutant detective. Directions, follow-up questions, and suggestions for extension projects.

Send: Your name and address on school stationery
Or call: The RCRA Hotline at 1-800-424-9346
Request: The Student Activity Sheets for Drinking Water Projects
Send to: U.S. Environmental Protection Agency
Information Access Branch
Public Information Center (PIC) 3404
401 M St. SW, #3404
Washington, DC 20460

Wasteful Thinking

"Solid waste awareness" is the goal, and this 145-page curriculum guide provides all the tools needed to achieve that end. Concentrating on math, science, and language arts, students investigate all aspects of garbage from creation to decomposition. Detailed lesson plans indicate clear learning objectives. Includes vocabulary lists, a play about garbage, cartoons and other reproducibles, resources for additional materials, and a bibliography for further research.

Send: Your name and address on school stationery
Or call: The RCRA Hotline at 1-800-424-9346
Request: A copy of *Let's Recycle: A Curriculum for Solid Waste Awareness*
Send to: U.S. Environmental Protection Agency
      Information Access Branch
      Public Information Center (PIC) 3404
      401 M St. SW, #3404
      Washington, DC 20460

Garbage!

A mere 17 percent of our garbage finds its way back into the recycling loop; there's still a lot to be done in terms of education regarding this important issue. Do your part to spread the word about recycling with the help of these 500 *Recycle It!* brochures. Lots of facts about plastics, how to recycle, and why it matters.

Send: Your name, address, and school name
Request: 500 copies of the brochure *Recycle It!*
Send to: The Soap and Detergent Association
      475 Park Ave. South
      New York, NY 10016

Caring Counts

KIND News Junior contains puzzles, games, trading cards, profiles of child stars, contests, and fun facts to encourage a caring attitude toward all living creatures (KIND stands for Kids In Nature's Defense). You can receive a sample preview issue (in a classroom pack with 32 copies!) at no cost.

Send: Your name and address on school stationery
Or fax: 203-434-9579
Request: A sample preview issue of *KIND News Junior*
Send to: The Publishers of *KIND News*
P.O. Box 362
East Haddam, CT 06423-0362

Garbage Gremlin

The EPA's pernicious Garbage Gremlin character leads the way through a comic book intended to explain the process of recycling to kids in grades four through seven. Students are encouraged to discuss the "cycle" of garbage, the problem of where to put the mountains of refuse produced each day, and the alternatives available for reusing a variety of materials. Eighteen pages with math puzzles, word games, and a mini-poster.

Send: Your name and address on school stationery
Or call: The RCRA Hotline at 1-800-424-9346
Request: A copy of *The Adventures of the Garbage Gremlin* comic book
Send to: U.S. Environmental Protection Agency
Information Access Branch
Public Information Center (PIC) 3404
401 M St. SW, #3404
Washington, DC 20460

Refuse Rider

Created by the Environmental Protection Agency and the National Science Teachers Association, this colorful poster first appeared in *The Science Teacher* magazine. It features the EPA's recurring Garbage Gremlin character being vanquished by a conscientious young recycler surfing "the wave of the future."

Send: Your name and address on school stationery
Or call: The RCRA Hotline at 1-800-424-9346
Request: The *Ride the Wave of the Future: Recycle Today!* poster
Send to: U.S. Environmental Protection Agency
Information Access Branch
Public Information Center (PIC) 3404
401 M St. SW, #3404
Washington, DC 20460

Resin Roundup

The type of resin they're made from is what distinguishes the various plastics. Kids can learn all about resin in this plastics reference guide. Designed for students in grades three and four, the kit explains how plastics are made and used, the Plastic Container Coding System (what the letters on the bottles mean about resin content), and what kids can do to recycle plastics.

Send: $2 (check or money order payable to Keep America Beautiful)
Request: Plastics Recycling by the Numbers
Send to: Keep America Beautiful
Mill River Plaza
9 West Broad St.
Stamford, CT 06902

Our National Heritage

An incredible one-third of the land in the United States is administered by the federal government. That means one-third of the country is public land, belonging to all Americans! This 15-page activity guide is designed to educate kids about what public lands are, our responsibilities regarding them, and how we can preserve the many parks, refuges, and forests for future generations.

Send: A self-addressed stamped envelope (#10)
Request: Preserving Our National Heritage
Send to: Keep America Beautiful
Mill River Plaza
9 West Broad St.
Stamford, CT 06902

Solar Power!

Using little more than a few pieces of cardboard and aluminum foil, discover how you can create an unforgettable science experiment your kids can eat! With this simple set of plans you can build an effective solar-powered hot dog cooker. You'll leave a lasting impression with your students regarding the power of our most readily observable energy source.

Send: A self-addressed stamped envelope and $.25
Request: The Solar Hot Dog Cooker Plan
Send to: Energy Management Center
P.O. Box 190
Port Richey, FL 34673

Lowdown on Litter

Why do people litter? Ignorance? Lack of respect or concern for their world? This simple brochure is packed with ideas for classroom discussion. It talks to kids about the attitudes and behavior that lead to careless littering and how littering affects others. Also covered are the seven main sources of litter and simple, concrete ways kids can have a major impact on the litter around them.

Send: A self-addressed stamped envelope (#10)
Request: Tips for Preventing Litter in Your Community
Send to: Keep America Beautiful
      Mill River Plaza
      9 West Broad St.
      Stamford, CT 06902

Leave No Trace!

That's the catchphrase for the Wilderness Society's education program designed to illustrate for kids the impact individual actions can have on a forest ecosystem. This colorful $31'' \times 21''$ poster shows the country's federal land and wilderness areas and includes an inset of all the nation's park service sites. There's even a special quiz (answers come from the map info), plus two visual find-the-problem puzzles.

Send: Your name and address
Request: The U.S. Federal Lands and Wilderness
Areas Map
Send to: The Wilderness Society
      Publications
      900 17th St. NW
      Washington, DC 20006-2596

SOS

Save Our Species is the subject of this publication from the EPA's Endangered Species Protection Program. Its 25 pages feature detailed blackline drawings of endangered or threatened plants and animals. Each species profile includes an informative paragraph of little-known facts, a national habitat map, and a small color portrait of the plant or animal. For students in grades K through six.

Send: Your name and address on school stationery
Or call: The RCRA Hotline at 1-800-424-9346
Request: A copy of *Endangered Species Coloring Book: Save Our Species*
Send to: U.S. Environmental Protection Agency
   Endangered Species Protection Program
   401 M St. SW
   Washington, DC 20460

Mister Rogers Recycles

This activity guide introduces young children to the important issues associated with the three R's (reduce, reuse, and recycle) in that special way only Mister Rogers can! It can help kids develop environmentally conscious attitudes early on. Also included are the words and music to Mister Rogers's recycling songs.

Send: $3 (check or money order payable to Keep America Beautiful)
Request: *Mister Rogers' Activity Book for Young Children*
Send to: Keep America Beautiful
   Mill River Plaza
   9 West Broad St.
   Stamford, CT 06902

America the Beautiful

Keep America Beautiful was working to improve the aesthetic quality of our public places long before it was politically correct to be concerned with "the environment." The message seems all the more important today. Spark some community pride in your students with this colorful poster celebrating Keep America Beautiful Month (which is April). It offers 30 environmental tips and ideas for kids to use each day.

Send: A self-addressed stamped envelope (#10)
Request: The Keep America Beautiful Month poster
Send to: Keep America Beautiful
Mill River Plaza
9 West Broad St.
Stamford, CT 06902

Public Property

The Wilderness Society's 60-year history of coordinating actions to protect our nation's public lands has produced a wealth of information. You can access a huge variety of materials for nominal fees. Dozens of 50- to 100-page reports by leading conservation scientists discuss everything from old-growth forests to the Everglades and cost just $3 to $5. Myriad ideas for integrating many subjects.

Send: Your name and address
Request: The Wilderness Society publications listing
Send to: The Wilderness Society
Publications
900 17th St. NW
Washington, DC 20006-2596

It's been calculated that all the usable freshwater on the planet amounts to a mere 0.7 percent of the world's total H_2O. The majority (99.3 percent) is to be found either in frozen icecaps or the salty oceans. With this in mind, it's easy to see the importance of understanding water, its essential properties, and how we can use our available water resources most effectively to ensure the continued integrity of the earth's vital hydrologic cycle. This intensive 60-page curriculum guide examines the scientific data about water, methods for maintaining water quality, water consumption, the treatment of water after use, the disposal of potentially contaminated waters, water reuse as an alternative to source development, and the causes of floods and drought. It provides a detailed analysis of the hydrologic cycle and conclusions about the management of water resources, along with a complete collection of teacher tools, quizzes, vocabulary lists, activities, reproducibles, and much more. Compiled by teaching professionals from around the country and sponsored by the National Council for Geography Education as part of the *Pathways in Geography* series, a continuing effort to bring geography into the lives of students at all levels.

Send: $5 (check or money order payable to the National Council for Geographic Education)
Request: *Water in the Global Environment*
Send to: The National Council for Geographic Education
16A Leonard Hall
Indiana University of Pennsylvania
Indiana, PA 15705-1087

Arbor Day History

Arbor Day creator J. Sterling Morton's legacy of steward-ship and environmental awareness has inspired nature lovers for 100 years. This beautiful, full-color poster (a big 22″ × 34″) tells the fascinating history of Arbor Day through words and pictures. Included is an authentic portrait of J. Sterling Morton that looks down over his own immortal words, "Other holidays repose upon the past; Arbor Day proposes for the future."

Send: Your name and address on school stationery
Request: *Arbor Day: A Celebration of Stewardship* poster
Send to: The National Arbor Day Foundation
Education Department
100 Arbor Ave.
Nebraska City, NE 68410

Celebrate Trees!

Since its creation more than 100 years ago, Arbor Day has become one of the most celebrated holidays on the planet. Millions of people around the world hold ceremonies, both simple and elaborate, all equal in their value to the mission of reforesting the earth. This comprehensive 25-page guide is filled with everything you need to prepare an Arbor Day commemoration that involves your whole community.

Send: Your name and address on school stationery
Request: *The Celebrate Arbor Day* guide
Send to: The National Arbor Day Foundation
Education Department
100 Arbor Ave.
Nebraska City, NE 68410

Hands-on study of the natural world can present endless possibilities for integrating a full spectrum of subject matter, from reading and creative writing to chemistry and astronomy. It's an effective way to engage students and has been shown to improve retention of learned material. The "living classroom" is a central ideal in the mission of the Roger Tory Peterson Institute. Through various instructor training programs, seminars, publications, and awards for outstanding innovation in individual curricula the Institute promotes the goal of a national program that will involve students, teachers, and communities in long-term studies of their immediate environments as tools for relating to a wide range of subjects. To learn more about incorporating nature into your teaching check out *Cornerstone: Dialogues on Teaching About Nature*, and the *Guide to the Roger Tory Peterson Institute of Natural History*, both with lots of ideas for activities and additional resource suggestions. The *Birds, Bats & Butterflies* newsletter provides ongoing support with a series of kid-friendly science experiments, lots of background science facts, and specific techniques related to setting up an effective nature study program.

Send: Your name and address
Or fax: 716-665-3794
Request: Teacher resource materials: *Guide; Cornerstone; Birds, Bats & Butterflies*
Send to: Roger Tory Peterson Institute
       311 Curtis St.
       Jamestown, NY 14701-9620

Get the Facts

Simple, straightforward, and jam-packed with information you can use, the Wilderness Society's Fact Sheets provide pages of nonstop conservation news. From Ansel Adams to wildlife refuges, these double-sided info sheets offer details about animals and public lands from coast to coast. History, logistics, scientific data, and critical issues facing dozens of diverse environments.

Send: Your name and address (preferably on school stationery)
Request: The Wilderness Society Fact Sheets
Send to: The Wilderness Society
Publications
900 17th St. NW
Washington, DC 20006-2596

Sierra Source

Founded by the renowned naturalist John Muir over a hundred years ago, the Sierra Club still stands at the forefront of conservation action. Its dozens of educational publications touch on all aspects of wilderness from forest fires to wetlands. Lots of ideas for classroom discussions, projects, and more, with most publications only $.50. An issue of *Sierra* magazine, with its stunning photos of wild places, costs $2.

Send: Your name and address
Or fax: 415-776-0350
Request: Sierra Club Environmental Resources List
Send to: Sierra Club
Department SA
P.O. Box 7586
San Francisco, CA 94120

Sail on Calypso!

Leaf through the pages of these beautiful publications and you'll find you can almost hear the familiar theme music, smell the salt of the sea, and feel warmed by the sincerity of the legendary French-accented voice that helped interest generations in the secret life of our planet's oceans. Millions of people worldwide fondly remember the perennially popular *Undersea World of Jacques Cousteau*. The Cousteau family has never wavered in its lifelong dedication to educating the earth's inhabitants about the precious gift of the world's oceans.

You can take your class right down into the sea's depths with the crew of the *Calypso* through the vivid photographs and detailed articles offered up in each issue of the *Dolphin Log*. Kids can learn about the lives of children from distant cultures, discover the individual traits of a diverse range of sea creatures, or simply enjoy the Cousteau Adventures comic book section. Puzzles, games, answers to kid's questions, and activities such as folding origami sea rays, are certain to engage your class and help instill a love for the natural world.

For a more adult perspective you'll also get a look at the *Calypso Log* and more serious investigations of the environmental issues that affect us all.

Send: $1 to help defray postage costs on materials
Request: The Cousteau Society Teacher Information Packet
Send to: The Cousteau Society
 870 Greenbriar Circle, Suite 402
 Chesapeake, VA 23320-2641

True Identity

Learning the names and characteristics of the different trees that surround us is a rewarding class experience. Students can conduct their own field research, make pressed leaf books, collect cones or seed pods, or involve themselves in reading, science, environmental studies, and much more. The Arbor Day Foundation's detailed 75-page field guide to trees is an exceptional tool for accurately identifying your neighborhood forest.

Send: Your name and address on school stationery
Request: *What Tree Is That?* (Specify the East/Central or Western version)
Send to: The National Arbor Day Foundation
Education Department
100 Arbor Ave.
Nebraska City, NE 68410

Old Growth

They've probably all heard the phrase by now, but how can you give your students a true sense of what the term "old-growth" really means? Try the Wilderness Society's *Wild, Wild World of Old-Growth Forests: A Teacher's Guide.* The 28-page publication illustrates that an old-growth forest is far more than just mossy old trees.

Send: $4 (check or money order payable to the Wilderness Society)
Request: *The Wild, Wild World of Old-Growth Forests: A Teacher's Guide*
Send to: The Wilderness Society
Publications
900 17th St. NW
Washington, DC 20006-2596

Children all over the globe have gone wild for Koko the gorilla. Her story can be the springboard for classroom discussions on topics as varied as sign language or the future of the rain forest. The 23-year-old Koko possesses the most advanced language skills of any non-human on the planet and the many televised and published accounts of her activities have inspired both gifted and special needs children to a greater intensity of interest in their studies. You can use the theme to enhance reading skills, explore earth science, investigate environmental issues, raise awareness about endangered species, or instigate a geographic adventure. The Gorilla Foundation provides an array of materials to support such activities, including gorilla fact sheets, ape language quiz games, and posters of the famous Koko. "Action Projects" encourage both kids and teachers to get involved by starting recycling programs, participating in Earth Day celebrations, holding conservation fairs, or writing letters to politicians. There are also lots of ideas for fundraisers to help the class join Koko's family (a $20 membership) and create an ongoing project.

Send: Your name and address
Or call: 1-800-634-6273
Request: The Teacher Information Pack
Send to: The Gorilla Foundation
             P.O. Box 620-530
             Woodside, CA 94062

Seasonal Forest

Just investigating the concept of deciduous vegetation can make for a lively classroom discussion. This detailed 15-page study guide offers lots of information about the important differences between deciduous and coniferous forests. Students can discover what kinds of animals depend on the cycles of the deciduous forest, where deciduous forests are found, and the effects seasonal changes have on this ecosystem.

Send: $2 (check or money order payable to the Bronx Zoo)
Request: *Deciduous Forests* (The Windows on Wildlife Series)
Send to: Education Department
Bronx Zoo/Wildlife Conservation Park
Bronx, NY 10460

The Lone Prairie

Plains, prairies, pampas, savannas—you might think they're all the same, but each is a distinct type of grassland with its own unique combination of plants and animals. Grasslands are an often overlooked natural environment that your students can learn all about in this 15-page study guide filled with photos, maps, and science facts. Also includes a glossary and bibliography.

Send: $2 (check or money order payable to the Bronx Zoo)
Request: *Grasslands* (The Windows on Wildlife Series)
Send to: Education Department
Bronx Zoo/Wildlife Conservation Park
Bronx, NY 10460

Rain Forest Report

Far more than just tangled jungles, the world's rain forests are unique ecosystems filled with creatures unlike those found anywhere else in nature. Through this detailed 15-page study guide, students can learn about the differences between a rain forest and a jungle, why the survival of the rain forest is vital to all life on earth, and the wide variety of animals and plants a rain forest supports.

Send: $2 (check or money order payable to the Bronx Zoo)
Request: *Rain Forests* (The Windows on Wildlife Series)
Send to: Education Department
      Bronx Zoo/Wildlife Conservation Park
      Bronx, NY 10460

Extinct Is Forever

Here's a nicely comprehensive introduction to endangered species for kids in the middle grade levels. Lots of good whole-language reading material, interesting details about individual endangered species, a well-rounded synopsis of the subject from the meaning of extinction to what individual kids can do to make a difference, plus a glossary and bibliography of additional resources where kids can find information about other environmental issues.

Send: $2 (check or money order payable to the Bronx Zoo)
Request: *Endangered Species*
(The Windows on Wildlife Series)
Send to: Education Department
      Bronx Zoo/Wildlife
      Conservation Park
      Bronx, NY 10460

Desert Life

Your students will never again think of deserts as endless barren sand dunes once they've seen this comprehensive study guide. Its 15 pages are filled with desert facts (how plants store water, which animals really live in the desert), articles about specific flora and fauna, photos, plus a glossary and bibliography. Produced by the New York Zoological Society as part of a continuing educational program.

Send: $2 (check or money order payable to the Bronx Zoo)
Request: *Deserts* (The Windows on Wildlife Series)
Send to: Education Department
      Bronx Zoo/Wildlife Conservation Park
      Bronx, NY 10460

Rivers Run

Our freshwater river systems are one of the most precious natural resources on the planet; their preservation is a matter of importance to every citizen. Introduce your students to the conservation concerns surrounding America's waterways with a sample issue of *American Rivers*. There are lots of river facts, articles about specific rivers, photos of famous supporters, plus ideas for getting involved with your own local rivers.

Send: Your name and address
Or fax: 202-543-6142
Request: Teacher information and a sample of *American Rivers*
Send to: American Rivers
      801 Pennsylvania Ave. SE, Suite 400
      Washington, DC 20003

More than 300 National Park Service units around the country provide thousands of interpretive educational programs each year with an emphasis not only on the natural wonders of a wilderness location, but also on the reasons why responsible stewardship of these national treasures is so important. In keeping with a long-standing tradition of cooperation between federal and state conservation experts, this 90-page archaeology resource guide from the U.S. Park Service's division of national preservation programs illustrates how educators can use state-run recreational facilities and locally available state scientists to create cooperative interpretive projects for the benefit of the schoolchildren from all regions of the country. Archaeology education programs from Montana, Nebraska, Colorado, Illinois, Iowa, Kansas, Missouri, New Mexico, North Dakota, Oklahoma, South Dakota, Texas, Wyoming, and even Saskatchewan, Canada, are examined in detail, focusing on which techniques worked and which didn't, so teachers can learn from each other's hard-earned insights. Candid evaluations of each state's programs can help you avoid the same mistakes, or exploit successful ideas. Includes how-to instructions for securing sponsors for archaeology events, organizing simulated "digs," involving the larger community in your efforts, printing materials, and more.

Send: Your name and address on school stationery
Request: A copy of *State Archaeological Education Programs*
Send to: U.S. Department of the Interior
National Park Service
Archaeological Assistance Program
P.O. Box 37127
Washington, DC 20013-7127

Humpback Ho!

Immerse your students in an expedition in search of one of the world's most magnificent creatures, the humpback whale! You can be on the cutting edge of marine mammal research and whale conservation studies, following migration routes, discovering each known whale's personality traits, even learning to recognize the unique white tail markings scientists have used to identify individuals.

The Whale Adoption Project is a program of the International Wildlife Coalition, an organization dedicated to protecting a variety of threatened animal species (whales dolphins, porpoises, seals, and others) and promoting research that will help ensure their continued survival. To increase awareness about marine mammals the IWC has created the *Whales of the World Teacher Kit*, an exceptionally comprehensive introduction to all the world's many species of whales. It includes not only scientific background information, whale facts, whale biology, history, etc., but there are also dozens of useful classroom reproducibles that integrate the whale theme with any course of study. Puzzles, word search games, diagrams, pictorials, articles on individual whales complete with photos, mazes, several pop quizzes, suggested activities, and even an extra-credit research project will give you everything you need to prepare many hours of lesson plans!

Send: $2 (check or money order payable to the Whale Adoption Project)
Request: *Whales of the World Teacher Kit*
Send to: Whale Adoption Project
        70 East Falmouth Hwy.
        East Falmouth, MA 02536-5954

KIND Kids

Tap into your older students' increasing interest in the world around them with the informative articles, profiles, puzzles, games, activities, contests, riddles, cartoons, environmental tips, quizzes, animal facts, and photos in each monthly issue of *KIND News Senior* (for students ages 12 through 18). This Kids In Nature's Defense publication is designed to incorporate math, language arts, reading, science, and more. Free sample classroom pack contains 32 copies.

Send: Your name and address on school stationery
Or fax: 203-434-9579
Request: A sample preview issue of *KIND News Senior*
Send to: The Publishers of *KIND News*
        P.O. Box 362
        East Haddam, CT 06423-0362

Sea Cow Primer

Introduce your primary-grade students to complex subjects like marine biology, environmental studies, and species conservation through this unique manatee coloring book. Students can strengthen their reading skills and increase environmental awareness with the engaging activities and reproducible drawings. Use the endearing manatees as a theme to help integrate reading, science, history, or even math as you discuss the manatees' dwindling numbers and the concept of extinction.

Send: Your name and address (on school stationery)
Request: *Manatees: A Coloring and Activity Book*
Send to: Save the Manatee Club
        500 North Maitland Ave., Suite 210
        Maitland, FL 32751

Science & Math

Cosmic Cartographers

On isolated mountaintops around the world the giant mirrored eyes of powerful telescopes peer deep into the darkest reaches of outer space. From earthbound observatories such as Palomar, Kitt Peak, and the Anglo-Australian come astonishing photos that most people never have the opportunity to see. They show a wondrous architecture of galaxies, stars, nebulae, planets, moons, and all the glittering lights in between. No less impressive are the images sent back by manned spacecraft, Skylab, orbiting satellites, the now functioning Hubble Space Telescope, and the unmanned Voyager probe.

Spark your students' interest in these exotic cosmic formations with the help of the Hansen Planetarium Space Science Library and Museum's collection of posters, postcards, slides, and booklets. Kids will marvel at the full-color photos and illustrations depicting the stunning landmarks astronomers have discovered in our universe. Prices for Hansen publications are very modest and can be as low as $1 for sale posters. Postcards start at just $.10 and are great for putting together a complete space portfolio. The hundreds of choices are always changing. Write for the latest price list, currently available selections, or samples of the items that might interest you.

Send: Your name and address on school stationery
Request: The latest publications information and/or appropriate samples
Send to: Hansen Planetarium Publications
        1845 South 300 West, #A
        Salt Lake City, UT 84115-1804

Earth Imagery

What does your state look like from space? How small a detail can orbiting satellites pick up? Your students will discover the answers to those questions and many more as they ponder the images on these posters from NASA and the NCGA. A set of two 18″ × 24″ posters includes four infrared and real color shots of various geographic features. Extremely precise explanations are found on the back of each poster.

Send: $3 (check or money order payable to the National Council for Geographic Education)
Request: Set of two NASA Image Posters
Send to: The National Council for Geographic Education
      16A Leonard Hall
      Indiana University of Pennsylvania
      Indiana, PA 15705-1087

Do-It-Yourself Orbiter

Build this authentic 1:1200 scale model of the U.S. space shuttle orbiter with your students while they read about the varied missions that the shuttle was designed to perform. The detailed instructions for assembly include lots of background on the shuttle: the purpose of its reusable parts, its place in the future of space transportation, and tips on getting your shuttle glider to fly successfully!

Send: Your name and address on school stationery
Request: The U.S. space shuttle glider kit
Send to: See "NASA Addresses," pages 146-147

We Have Liftoff!

Developed by NASA with the help of *Science Weekly*, the Operation Liftoff program's series of workbooks was designed as an introduction to space travel for students in grades one through three. The four activity guides are titled *Living in Space*, *Astronomy*, *Space Transportation*, and *Space Futures*. Each 50-page booklet contains dozens of math exercises, science experiments, vocabulary lists, and more.

Send: Your name and address on school stationery
Request: The Operation Liftoff Elementary Space Program series of resource guides with activities
Send to: See "NASA Addresses," pages 146-147

Planetary Puzzle

NASA's 30-plus years of photographing the solar system with an army of spacecraft, orbiters, probes, and landers has resulted in volumes of pictures. That vast collection was used to compile the drawings for this solar system puzzle. The complete kit of reproducibles allows you to provide a puzzle for each student, complete with detailed directions for realistic planet colors.

Send: Your name and address on school stationery
Request: The Solar System Puzzle Kit
Send to: See "NASA Addresses," pages 146-147

Is it possible that people will one day live and work most of their lives in orbiting scientific laboratories? Will we escape from our own solar system to inhabit other planets? For the 24,000 members of the National Space Society there is no doubt, and their mission is to support the colonization of space in every way possible. The NSS board of governors boasts such luminaries as Hugh Downs, Jacques Cousteau, Majel Barrett Roddenberry, and Arthur C. Clarke, as well as prominent govenment members including house speaker Newt Gingrich and former astronaut John Glenn, plus several other experienced NASA astronauts and internationally respected scientists. Space exploration can be an alluring subject for students, engaging their interest in many ways. Intersecting with language arts, mathematics, science, and physics, the subject of life in space is a great focal point for interdisciplinary teaching. Students can read all about the cutting edge of "creating a spacefaring civilization," in the official National Space Society magazine *Ad Astra* (Latin for "to the stars"). NSS-sponsored activities around the country include teacher workshops, school demonstrations, student seminars, and simulated space missions, many made available through cooperative ventures with NASA, the National Science Teachers Association, the Challenger Center, and others.

Send: Your name and address on school stationery
Request: National Space Society information for teachers and a preview issue of *Ad Astra*
Send to: National Space Society
The International Space Center
922 Pennsylvania Ave. SE
Washington, DC 20003-2140

Planet Hopping

With their customary cleverness the NASA scientists have created a board game for primary grade kids that combines math, science, astronomy, and more. Students color the 11" × 24" solar system, then take turns choosing cards with instructions like "go to the planet with the most rings" or "hitch a ride on a comet." Teachers are encouraged to make multiple copies of the game for playing in smaller groups.

Send: Your name and address on school stationery
Request: *Planet Hopping: A Gameboard for the Primary Student*
Send to: See "NASA Addresses," pages 146-147

Rocketry

In this 45-page introduction to rockets, NASA scientists share their expertise through a dozen simple experiments that illustrate how mathematics, chemistry, physical science, technology education, and Newton's Laws all relate to rocket science. Designed for use in grades two through six, this comprehensive activity guide features extensive background information, unusual historical facts, and clear explanations of rocket technology. Includes materials lists, vocabulary words, and suggestions for further study.

Send: Your name and address on school stationery
Request: *Rockets: Physical Science Teacher's Guide with Activities*
Send to: See "NASA Addresses," pages 146-147

NASA Notes

Your students can learn all about the practical side of life in space. They can take a personal tour through the space shuttle orbiter's systems, examine the logistics of living in space, learn how an astronaut's pressure suit works, and see inside the vehicles and facilities that make a shuttle launch possible. Fascinating Information Summaries from NASA cover these topics and much more. Dozens of titles.

Send: Your name and address on school stationery
Request: A selection of NASA Information Summaries
Send to: See "NASA Addresses," pages 146-147

Look Before You LEAP

The U.S. Park Service network represents an immense reservoir of field experts, ecologists, biologists, archaeologists, and other scientific professionals, all ready to share their knowledge. The 235-page *Listing of Education in Archaeological Programs* (LEAP) is a directory to those experts and the materials they create. It catalogs a wealth of classroom presentations, school curricula, videos, posters, and other educational aids related to the study of archaeology.

Send: Your name and address on school stationery
Request: The LEAP Directory
Send to: U.S. Department of the Interior
National Park Service
Archaeological Assistance Program
P.O. Box 37127
Washington, DC 20013-7127

Living Classroom

Even hard-to-reach kids respond to the living classroom's natural appeal. Plant your own wildflower meadow and augment science, creative writing, and even math skills. This annual mix lets you try your hand without a long-term commitment! Enough for a 125-square foot patch of vibrant color. The catalog has lots of tips on successful wildflower gardening.

Send: $5 (check or money order payable to the Vermont Wildflower Farm)
Request: The ½-ounce annual wildflower mix and latest Vermont Wildflower Farm catalog
Send to: The Vermont Wildflower Farm
　　　　Route 7
　　　　Charlotte, VT 05445

Pondering Plants

A living garden center with interrelated activities can help you reach difficult students, engage ESL or special needs children, and improve the level of interest and participation for every kid in class. This 14-minute video presentation lets you see the plant-based curriculum concept in action.

Send: $5 (check or money order payable to The National Gardening Association)
Request: Introductory video: *GrowLab: A Growing Experience*
Send to: The National Gardening Association
　　　　Education Department
　　　　180 Flynn Ave.
　　　　Burlington, VT 05401

Growing Ideas

According to formal evaluations performed for the National Science Foundation, students whose classroom learning incorporated live plant experiment stations actually scored higher than other students when tested for conceptual understanding, investigatory skills, and a positive attitude toward science in general. Botanical learning centers can provide a central theme for teaching subjects as diverse as language arts and statistical mathematics. The National Gardening Association's educator newsletter, *Growing Ideas*, provides ongoing support for your newly emerging classroom plant laboratory. It's filled with proven techniques shared by teaching professionals from around the country that will help with the logistics of selecting a location, collecting supplies, or planning lessons. It also offers lots of ideas for integrated activities that can relate to any subject in your curriculum. You can receive a free introductory packet of information that includes a sample pack of seeds to get you started and an informative eight-page booklet with practical advice on how to secure grants or other community funding for the purchase of your complete plant laboratory.

Send: Your name and address
Or call: 1-800-538-7476
Request: The GrowLab introductory packet with sample seeds and a preview issue of *Growing Ideas*
Send to: The National Gardening Association
        Education Department
        180 Flynn Ave.
        Burlington, VT 05401

Dig This

This 42-page collection of six programs excerpted from a national education symposium provides teachers with practical applications that will allow them to utilize the science of archaeology in their classrooms. For all grades.

Send: Your name and address on school stationery
Request: *Archaeology and Education: The Classroom and Beyond*
Send to: U.S. Department of the Interior
National Park Service
Archaeological Assistance Program
P.O. Box 37127
Washington, DC 20013-7127

Focus on Science

Each issue of the quarterly newsletter *Focus on Science Education* concentrates on a central theme that is explored from the perspectives of the various disciplines represented within the California Academy of Sciences network. Kids see subjects through the "focus" articles by zoologists, entomologists, mammalogists, botanists, astronomers, and other experts. The 12 information-packed pages include puzzles, interviews, experiments, vocabulary words, and hands-on activities. Ask for a free sample issue.

Send: A large 9″×12″ self-addressed stamped envelope
Request: A sample issue of *Focus on Science Education* newsletter
Send to: *Focus on Science Education*
The California Academy of Sciences
Golden Gate Park
San Francisco, CA 94118

Art to Zoo

The Smithsonian Education Department has drawn on its legendary natural history resources to produce this ongoing series of activity guides entitled *Art to Zoo*. Each issue focuses on a central theme and explores that subject from many perspectives: historical, biological, social, and artistic. Lots of background information, vocabulary words, specific activities, discussion ideas, poems, a bilingual section, and suggestions for continuing study.

Send: Your name, address, and school name
Request: *Art to Zoo*
Send to: Office of Elementary and Secondary Education
Arts and Industries Building
1163/MRC 402
Smithsonian Institution
Washington, DC 20560

Bubble Basics

Produced in cooperation with the Chicago Children's Museum, this 16-page bubble activity book illustrates a variety of scientific principles using the properties of one of kids' favorite playthings. Students piece together the booklets, which are filled with bubble puzzles, mazes, experiments, bubble magic tricks, even bubble art. Also includes a recipe for making your own inexpensive bubble stuff. For ages six through ten.

Send: Your name and address with school name
Request: *The Art and Science of Bubbles* (You can request enough for your whole class.)
Send to: The Soap and Detergent Association
475 Park Ave. South
New York, NY 10016

Airport Report

Designed to be used as a six-lesson unit for the instruction of middle-school students, this 56-page curriculum guide offers an appropriately complex investigation of the earth's atmosphere. Includes background facts and experiments; an analysis of the mechanics of airplane flight, pilot training, and airplane instruments; and an examination of how an airport works, including air traffic control functions.

Send: Your name and address on school stationery
Request: *Safety in the Air*
Send to: FAA Great Lakes Region
Aviation Education Program
2300 East Devon, Room 434
Des Plaines, IL 60018

Kinder-Science

Even kindergarten kids can be introduced to basic science, and that's what this comprehensive curriculum guide helps you do. Developed for students through third grade, the 260-page publication contains hundreds of activities, science experiments, reproducible worksheets, whole-language assignments, paper models, test questions, and an extensive index of related books for children. This is a must-see for K through three teachers.

Send: Your name and address on school stationery
Request: Aviation & Space Curriculum Guide, Grades K–3
Send to: FAA Great Lakes Region
Aviation Education Program
2300 East Devon, Room 434
Des Plaines, IL 60018

Metric Mandate

Though America has had a metric conversion program in place since 1975, 20 years later the internationally accepted standards of measurement are still not in general use in this country. In fact, the United States is the *only* country that does not officially use or teach the metric system! In 1875 the U.S. was one of the original signatory nations to an agreement called the Treaty of Meter, establishing standardized containers, quantities, lengths, weights, and thereby trade logistics around the globe. But the comfortable pound/inch system still persists.

By not understanding metrics Americans limit their ability to compete in a global market. As chief of the Metric Program at the National Institute of Standards and Technology, Dr. Gary Carver's ambition is to do away with his own job by making America completely metric. Give your students a head start on learning this easily understood system that we often use but don't officially teach. The Metric Program can provide you with a wealth of classroom tools: metric conversion cards or metric rulers for the entire class; giant metric posters; metric math problems; reproducibles with metric facts, comparison graphs, quizzes, and puzzles; and background information on the metric movement.

Send: Your name and address on school stationery
Request: The metric conversion teacher information pack
Send to: The Metric Program
        U.S. Department of Commerce
        National Institute of Standards and Technology
        Building 411, Room A-146
        Gaithersburg, MD 20899-0001

Water Trivia

How much water does it take to produce an ear of corn, a gallon of gasoline, or a fast-food meal? To manufacture a car or fuel a human being for the day? How big are raindrops? Send your students on a mathematical odyssey to investigate the multitude of uses and abuses endured by the world's freshwater supplies with these 53 surprising facts about the essential liquid.

Send: Your name and address on school stationery
Or call: The RCRA Hotline at 1-800-424-9346
Request: *Startling Statements* Activity Guide
Send to: U.S. Environmental Protection Agency
Information Access Branch
Public Information Center (PIC) 3404
401 M St. SW, #3404
Washington, DC 20460

Experiment Expo!

Wow! These four file folders can help you fill hours of classroom time with easy to re-create science experiments kids will participate in eagerly. Folders for the environment, communications, nonpowered flight, and space exploration are packed with dozens of useful exercises and activities relating science to aerospace technology and technology back to all basic science. A gold mine for upper elementary grade teachers!

Send: Your name and address on school stationery
Request: Demonstration Aids for Aviation Education
Send to: FAA Great Lakes Region
Aviation Education Program
2300 East Devon, Room 434
Des Plaines, IL 60018

With computer literacy now an essential component of every child's education, students need a basic understanding of the technology driving computer hardware. In an ambitious effort to support the increased computer literacy of students nationwide, Intel offers educators a hands-on means for explaining the internal workings of the personal computer. Designed by middle-school science and computer teachers, Intel engineers, and the International Society for Technology in Education, *Journey Inside: The Computer* is specifically for use with kids in grades five through nine and represents a gold mine of teaching tools. The box itself forms the shell of a PC that students can open and examine. It comes with a 300-page, six-week lesson plan containing extensive background information, vocabulary, activities, handouts, overheads, and more. A six-part video introduces each section and correlates with the full-color poster that provides constant reference. Perhaps most impressive is the "Chip Kit," an actual silicon wafer, microprocessor, and loose processor chips to examine and use in various electronics experiments! Simply return the official request application to receive this program (you must be a qualified math, science, or computer teacher for grades five through nine).

Send: Your name and address on school stationery
Request: An application form for *Journey Inside: The Computer* teacher materials kit
Send to: Intel Corporation
P.O. Box 7641
Mt. Prospect, IL
60056-7641

Wrapping up Math

Learning Wrap-Up boards were designed by a fourth-grade teacher to help her students learn basic math skills. The innovative idea combines elements of manual dexterity with self-correcting repetition exercises that encourage students to practice a variety of mathematical functions. So well-received they've been expanded into pre-algebra, language arts, ESL, and even science subjects. A free sample board lets you see the idea in action.

Send: Your name and address
Or call: 1-800-992-4966
Request: The Learning Wrap-Up intro pack with sample wrap-up
Send to: Learning Wrap-Ups
        2122 East 6550 South
        Ogden, UT 84405

Fractals and Tessellations

Students will view math in a whole new light when they see dramatic images of equations depicted visually in posters of fractals and tessellations by Dale Seymour. Astonishing shapes that absorb and intrigue are the norm here, including the work of artists such as M.C. Escher and realistic science posters. A myriad of materials covering mathematics, language arts, fine arts, visual thinking, and more.

Send: Your name and address on school stationery
Request: The latest Dale Seymour Posters catalog or the Dale Seymour Publications catalogs, Grades K–8 and 6–12
Send to: Dale Seymour Publications
        P.O. Box 10888
        Palo Alto, CA 94303-0878

Pressure Points

This curriculum guide is all about air, its observable properties, how we use our knowledge of air, how weather affects air, and lots more. Designed for use with kids in grades three through five, the 33-page publication provides dozens of science experiments with detailed instructions and materials lists, suggested activities, study questions, even helpful tips from fellow teachers.

Send: Your name and address on school stationery
Request: Aviation Science Activities for Elementary Grades
Send to: FAA Great Lakes Region
Aviation Education Program
2300 East Devon, Room 434
Des Plaines, IL 60018

Volcano Visuals

Study the mechanics of volcanism with this three-dimensional paper model designed to provide a graphic illustration of volcano structure and the causes of eruptions. Detailed instructions for construction include an easy-to-follow pattern, plus vocabulary terms, additional suggested readings, and study questions to encourage further research.

Send: $1.50 (check or money order payable to U.S. Geological Survey)
Request: Open-File Report 91-115A: *Make Your Own Paper Model of a Volcano*
Send to: Open-File Reports—ESIC
U.S. Geological Survey
Box 25286, Federal Center
Denver, CO 80225

Earth Notes

A compilation of activities collected from environmental science educators across the country, *Earth Notes* offers 16 pages of proven projects, experiments, and other hands-on ways to involve your students in an exploration of their local ecosystems. Includes ideas for scientific investigations such as tracking insects through their various stages and monitoring the seasonal changes at a favorite park. For use with grades K through six.

Send: Your name and address on school stationery
Or call: The RCRA Hotline at 1-800-424-9346
Request: A copy of *Earth Notes*
Send to: U.S. Environmental Protection Agency
   Earth Notes
   401 M St. SW
   Washington, DC 20460

Glacial Graphics

This kit contains complete instructions and templates for constructing two different three-dimensional models, a mountain valley partially filled with a glacier and the same valley after the glacier recedes. Illustrate how glaciers are formed and how their forces affect landscape features.

Send: $3 (check or money order payable to U.S. Geological Survey)
Request: Open-File Report 89-190A: *How to Construct Two Paper Models Showing the Effects of Glacial Ice on a Mountain Valley*
Send to: Open-File Reports—ESIC
   U.S. Geological Survey
   Box 25286, Federal Center
   Denver, CO 80225

Earthquake!

Slip faults, subduction faults, tremors, and aftershocks—
as earthquakes increase in frequency the language of seis-
mography slips into our everyday consciousness. How do
earthquakes occur? Why do they cause so much damage?
This paper model can help students visualize the causes of
an earthquake and its results. Includes a 22-page educator's guide with additional ideas and resources.

Send: $3 (check or money order payable to U.S. Geologi-
cal Survey)
Request: Open-Files Report 92-200A: *Earthquake Effects*
Send to: Open-File Reports—ESIC
        U.S. Geological Survey
        Box 25286, Federal Center
        Denver, CO 80225

Earth Forces

Colorful, informative wall decor is an asset for any classroom. This giant $54'' \times 41''$ map depicting the powerful geological features that shape our planet can help students
become familiar with a variety of important natural
forces. The computer-generated image shows all the
world's volcanoes, earthquakes, and major tectonic plates
in detail. Provides a great visual aid for integrating these
subjects and illustrating their influences on the land.

Send: $4 (check or money order payable to U.S. Geologi-
cal Survey)
Request: *This Dynamic Planet—World Map*
Send to: Branch of Distribution
        U.S. Geological Survey
        Box 25286, Federal Center
        Denver, CO 80225

Cloud Crazy!

Clouds captivate children and adults alike. You can capture your students' attention with this detailed cloud chart. Designed for grades three through five, it's a full-color 11″× 17″ poster that covers cloud shapes, the basics of weather patterns, and how winds make clouds, all illustrated by 19 captioned photos of various cloud formations. Forecasting secrets and lightning facts are also included.

Send: $2 (check or money order payable to Cloud Chart, Inc.)
Request: Cloud Chart C: Grades 3–5
Send to: Cloud Chart, Inc.
P.O. Box 21298
Charleston, SC 29413-1298

Weather Watching

Translate the language of clouds with this 11″× 17″ full-color poster depicting 35 different cloud formations, along with detailed descriptions of the wind patterns that create them and the impending weather events they forecast. Designed for grades six and up, this poster is approved by the National Science Teachers' Association and used in general science, geoscience, and meteorology courses worldwide.

Send: $2 (check or money order payable to Cloud Chart, Inc.)
Request: Cloud Chart B: Grades six and up
Send to: Cloud Chart, Inc.
P.O. Box 21298
Charleston, SC 29413-1298

Weather Wonders

Having trouble showing the difference between a nimbo-stratus and a stratocumulus cloud? Here's a big 17″× 22″ reference chart with 35 full-color photos of various cloud formations, including detailed captions about the winds that cause them and what they imply for the weather forecast. The same chart used in major encyclopedias, by weather bureaus worldwide, and even the FAA and American Meteorological Society.

Send: $3 (check or money order payable to Cloud Chart, Inc.)
Request: Cloud Chart A
Send to: Cloud Chart, Inc.
P.O. Box 21298
Charleston, SC 29413-1298

Planet Poster

Why are there craters on the moon? What other planets have mountains or volcanoes? Are there really shapes that look like pyramids on Mars? Examine the geological formations of the moon and the planets in our solar system with this large 35″× 48″ full-color poster. These are actual maps with distinguishing planetary and lunar features with detailed and descriptive explanations of the various recognizable surface formations.

Send: $1.50 (check or money order payable to U.S. Geological Survey)
Request: Planetary Maps
Send to: Branch of Distribution
U.S. Geological Survey
Box 25286, Federal Center
Denver, CO 80225

Dino History

This coloring book provides a fun format for introducing primary grade kids to dinosaurs and early earth history. When dinosaurs lived, what they ate, what they might have looked like are all presented in the simplest of language including fun facts and various follow-up ideas along with unique pictures to color. A great starting point for discussions on a variety of topics.

Send: $3.95 (check or money order payable to Bellerophon Books; CA residents add appropriate sales tax)
Request: #084-9: The Coloring Book of Dinosaurs
Send to: Bellerophon Books
         36 Anacapa St.
         Santa Barbara, CA 93101

Satellite View

Orbiting satellites give earth dwellers a whole new look at the multifaceted sphere that is our home. Detailed satellite photographs of geological features allow for an understanding of formations far too big to be studied from ground level. This 28″ × 19″ color satellite image taken over the continental United States is an excellent visual aid that comes complete with detailed descriptions of 24 visible natural features.

Send: $3.10 (check or money order payable to U.S. Geological Survey)
Request: U.S. Satellite View
Send to: Branch of Distribution
         U.S. Geological Survey
         Box 25286, Federal Center
         Denver, CO 80225

Sea World

A poignant quote from *Killer Whales* says, "for in the end we will conserve only what we love, we will love only what we understand, we will understand only what we are taught." Teaching is the impetus for this extensive collection of educational materials, dozens of teacher guides, booklets on various species, posters, videos, all $5–$15. Designed to integrate math, science, geography, art, and language. Ask for a free listing of materials.

Send: Your name and address
Or call: 1-800-23-SHAMU
Request: The official educational materials order form
Send to: Sea World Education Department
Attention: Educational Materials
1720 South Shores Rd.
San Diego, CA 92109-7995

Dolphin Facts

Though generational behavior studies have been done on both chimps and gorillas, no one before Dr. Denise Herzing had attempted such an extensive long-term project with a species from the world's ocean community. This fact sheet is packed with the fruits of ten years of her dedicated research efforts, featuring insights and details not previously known about the engaging spotted dolphins of the tropical Atlantic.

Send: Your name and address
Request: Introductory information packet and spotted dolphin fact sheet
Send to: The Wild Dolphin Project
P.O. Box 3839
Palos Verdes, CA 90274-9779

Studying Sirenia

You'll be amazed at the wealth of ideas, activities, reproducible study sheets, and other materials included in this
comprehensive curriculum guide to the fascinating manatee. Far more than just facts about manatee biology or history, this guide integrates discussions of the food chain,
human populations, hydrology, water usage, scientific tax-
onomy, geography, and much more. Also included is a
beautiful 22″ × 17″ full-color poster.

Send: Your name and address on school letterhead
Request: *Manatees: An Educator's Guide*
Send to: Save the Manatee Club
      500 North Maitland Ave., Suite 210
      Maitland, FL 32751

Sea Sirens

Dive into the world of the West Indian manatee with this
23-minute full-color videotape presentation about
Florida's gentle "mermaids" of the sea. Narrated by
Leonard Nimoy, this program describes the natural history
of the manatee in Florida and takes a look at the most
critical threat to the manatee's survival, the loss of its native habitat. Loaned, free of charge, for a two-week period.

Send: Your name and address on school letterhead
Request: The videocassette *Silent Sirens:
Manatees in Peril*
Send to: Save the Manatee Club
      500 North Maitland Ave.,
      Suite 210
      Maitland, FL 32751

NASA Addresses

For proper service, it's important to write to the NASA Teacher Resource Center nearest you to request the NASA items listed in this book. For this reason, each NASA entry refers you to this section for an address. An individual center can also provide the educators in its area with materials customized to specific classroom needs. Your regional NASA outreach program will also have a wealth of additional publications, computer software, video materials, and more.

Servicing: Alaska, Arizona, California, Hawaii, Idaho, Washington, Montana, Nevada, Oregon, Utah, and Wyoming

Education Programs Branch
Mail Stop 204-12
NASA Ames Research Center
Moffett Field, CA 94035-1000

Servicing: Connecticut, Maine, Massachusetts, New Jersey, Pennsylvania, Vermont, Delaware, Maryland, New Hampshire, New York, Rhode Island, and the District of Columbia

Educational Programs
Mail Code 130
NASA Goddard Space Flight Center
Greenbelt, MD 20771

Servicing: Colorado, Nebraska, North Dakota, South Dakota, Kansas, New Mexico, Oklahoma, and Texas

Education and Public Services Branch
Mail Code AP–4
NASA Johnson Space Center
Houston, TX 77058-3696

Servicing: Florida, Puerto Rico, Georgia, and the Virgin Islands

Education Services Branch
Mail Code PA-ESB
NASA Kennedy Space Center
Kennedy Space Center, FL 32899-0001

Servicing: Kentucky, South Carolina, West Virginia, North Carolina, and Virginia

Education Programs Office
Mail Stop 400
NASA Langley Research Center
Hampton, VA 23381-0001

Servicing: Illinois, Michigan, Ohio, Indiana, Minnesota, Wisconsin

Office of Educational Programs
Mail Stop 7–4
NASA Lewis Research Center
21000 Brookpark Road
Cleveland, OH 44135-3191

Servicing: Alabama, Iowa, Tennessee, Arkansas, Louisiana, and Missouri

Education Programs Office
Mail Code CL01
NASA Marshall Space Flight Center
Huntsville, AL 35812-0001

Servicing: Mississippi

Educational Programs
Mail Stop MA00
NASA Stennis Space Center
Stennis Space Center, MS 39529-6000

Also:

NASA Headquarters
Public Inquiries—Code POS
Washington, DC 20546

NASA Jet Propulsion Laboratory
Public Information Office—Code 180-200
Pasadena, CA 91109

Special Needs

Open Captions

Special-needs students can really enjoy mainstream inclusion with the help of these films and videos from Modern Talking Pictures. All have been modified for the hearing impaired with open captions, meaning no need for a decoder since the words appear right on screen. This generous program is made possible by the U.S. Department of Education, and it provides free loans of materials to all qualifying educators. The only requirement is that you have at least one hearing-impaired student currently in your charge. Two separate catalogs of available titles list nearly 5,000 films and videos for you to choose from. General interest topics cover after-school specials, outdoor adventure, and even the latest Hollywood releases; the catalog of educational programs covers all subjects—math, language arts, science, biology, and more—for preschool through high school students. Each educational program also includes a complete teacher lesson guide with additional illustrations, maps, diagrams, reproducibles, curriculum goals, a complete script, and tips on getting the most instructional value from the film or video presented. This is a free loan service; VHS videos even include a prepaid return postage label!

Send: Your name and address on school stationery
Request: The latest Educational Programs or General Interest catalog of captioned films and videos
Send to: Captioned Films/Videos
Modern Talking Picture Service, Inc.
5000 Park St. North
St. Petersburg, FL 33709

LD Demystified

Since the National Institutes of Health estimate that ten percent of the U.S. population has some form of learning disability, it's a fair bet you've had experience with children who were struggling to overcome a personal barrier. This 50-page packet provides a variety of informational tools that can help you better identify kids who may need special attention and better understand the nature of learning disabilities.

Send: Your name and address
Request: The General Information Packet on Learning Disabilities
Send to: The National Center for Learning Disabilities
      381 Park Ave. South, Suite 1420
      New York, NY 10016

What Did She Say?

Hearing impairment is a difficult problem to identify because there are few physical signs of the problem. But a child whose hearing is compromised exhibits a recognizable range of behaviors indicating he or she is not receiving the auditory information you are dispensing. These booklets and fact sheets are designed to help educators identify at-risk kids and modify classroom practices to allow hearing-impaired children to function effectively.

Send: Your name and address
Request: The information packet on education and the hearing impaired
Send to: The Better Hearing Institute
      P.O. Box 1840
      Washington, DC 20013

Learn Braille

These informative cards were designed to help raise awareness among sighted people about the use of Braille, large type print, and the mission of American Printing House for the Blind. The cards present a sample of large type, the complete Braille alphabet, and the history of APH. As a special educational service, APH makes these cards available free of charge (maximum of five copies per request).

Send: Your name and address
Or call: 1-800-223-1839
Request: APH Alphabet Card Folder
Send to: American Printing House
for the Blind
1839 Frankfort Ave.
Louisville, KY 40206-0085

Braille Reader

For kids ages eight and older, this special Braille/print version of the popular *My Weekly Reader* was created to be used by both blind readers and print readers in an effort to increase awareness about the unique obstacles facing students who are sight impaired. The information is presented in both Braille and print, side by side. Up to five copies are available free of charge.

Send: Your name and address
Or call: 1-800-223-1839
Request: *My Weekly Reader* Special Braille Edition
Send to: American Printing House for the Blind
1839 Frankfort Ave.
Louisville, KY 40206-0085

Sight Aid

American Printing House for the Blind has the most inclusive catalog of tools available to teachers of the sight impaired. APH manufactures books and magazines in Braille, large type, recorded, and computer disk form, plus all manner of daily living aids and other scholastic materials. The valuable 200-plus page sourcebook is free.

Send: Your name and address
Or call: 1-800-223-1839
Request: APH Catalog of Instructional Aids, Tools, and Supplies
Send to: American Printing House for the Blind
1839 Frankfort Ave.
Louisville, KY 40206-0085

Books to Hear

The National Library Service for the Blind and Physically Handicapped maintains an extensive collection of Braille, recorded books, and other materials for people with special needs (low vision, loss of sight, physical limitations). Service includes free loans of the playback equipment. To qualify you must have at least one student with certified impairment.

Send: Your name and address
Or call: 1-800-424-9100
Request: The introductory information package and application for service
Send to: The Reference Section
National Library Service for the Blind and
Physically Handicapped
Library of Congress
Washington, DC 20542

Products for Special Kids

It's always easier to do a job well with the proper tools, and this 100-page catalog of equipment for special-needs children can help you find just the right tool for dealing with the unique physical requirements of your exceptional students. Whether you need body support devices, play equipment, developmental toys, ambulatory aids, or other products for use by the physically challenged, Cleo has it.

Send: Your name and address
Or call: 1-800-321-0595
Request: The latest Cleo for Kids catalog
Send to: Cleo, Inc.
          3957 Mayfield Rd.
          Cleveland, OH 44121

Bilingual Science

For some students, science is a tough enough subject without the added pressures of a language barrier. This curriculum guide offers practical tips and techniques for creating a science program that will help your bilingual and ESL students to follow directions and effectively communicate the results of experiments. Designed to help teachers of grades four through eight, the 27-page publication includes proven activities and lesson plans.

Send: $3.50 (check or money order payable to The National Clearinghouse for Bilingual Education)
Request: Program Information Guide #11: *Teaching Science to English Learners Grades 4–8*
Send to: The National Clearinghouse for
          Bilingual Education
         1118 22nd St. NW
         Washington, DC 20037

Math Lingo

Math can be a real challenge for ESL students. This program suggests an integrated approach combining math and literacy instruction. Contains sample lessons, tips, and techniques from seasoned ESL specialists.

Send: $3.50 (check or money order payable to The National Clearinghouse for Bilingual Education)
Request: Program Information Guide #15: *Reforming Mathematics Instruction for ESL Literacy Students*
Send to: The National Clearinghouse for
　　　　　　Bilingual Education
　　　　　　1118 22nd St. NW
　　　　　　Washington, DC 20037

Word Workshop

It's not always necessary for young children to develop complete oral competency in their second language to perform effectively in a written environment. It appears that the combination of writing and speaking facilitates the acquisition of skills in both areas. For kids in grades K through six, this curriculum guide suggests writing workshops as study aids. It includes assessment strategies and a bibliography of additional resources.

Send: $3.50 (check or money order payable to The National Clearinghouse for Bilingual Education)
Request: Program Information Guide #10: *Writer's Workshop and Children Acquiring English as a Non-Native Language*
Send to: The National Clearinghouse for
　　　　　　Bilingual Education
　　　　　　1118 22nd St. NW
　　　　　　Washington, DC 20037

ESL Assessment

Though readily accessible, traditional standardized assessment programs do not always accurately reflect an individual ESL student's actual progress since there are language barrier factors that can affect the child's ability to understand the test itself. This 24-page curriculum guide reviews the bilingual testing dilemma in-depth and suggests less intimidating, alternative assessment approaches.

Send: $3.50 (check or money order payable to The National Clearinghouse for Bilingual Education)
Request: Program Information Guide #3: *Informal Assessment in Educational Evaluation: Implications for Bilingual Education Programs*
Send to: The National Clearinghouse for
Bilingual Education
1118 22nd St. NW
Washington, DC 20037

Special Needs

Tap into all the resources available for accommodating your special needs kids with the help of this guide to federal programs. Access information on all federal, state, or local services that apply to your specific situation.

Send: Your name and address on school stationery
Request: *Pocket Guide to Federal Help for Individuals with Disabilities*
Send to: The Clearinghouse on Disability Information
Office of Special Education and Rehabilitation
U.S. Department of Education
Room 3132, Switzer Building
Washington, DC 20202-2524

Helping Hands

Bilingual education, ESL, and sensitivity training are combined in this coloring book from the National Association for Humane and Environmental Education. It contains 35 pages of blackline reproducibles, each with a message in side-by-side English and Spanish. The theme is that family dog and cat pets depend on us for their survival, and the pictures illustrate why it's so important to show pets care and compassion at all times.

Send: $3 (check or money order payable to NAHEE)
Request: A copy of the bilingual coloring book *How To Be a Helping Hand to Dogs and Cats*
Send to: The National Association for Humane
and Environmental Education
P.O. Box 362
East Haddam, CT 06423-0362

Fun & Games

Stamp collecting can provide an interesting means to engage kids in a variety of subjects. This 15-page stamp finder offers a comprehensive introduction to philately, history, how to identify a stamp's country of origin, distinguishing important markings that affect a stamp's value, and the vocabulary of stamp collecting.

Send: $2 (check or money order payable to the Jamestown Stamp Company)
Request: The Harris Stamp Finder
Send to: Jamestown Stamp Company
341 East Third St.
Jamestown, NY 14701-0019

Have a Heart

Add that special touch to corrected papers, tests, or any student assignment with these friendly heart stickers. With this introductory offer from Treasure Toy House you get 100 stickers shaped like hearts, some red, some blue, all imprinted with a bright smiley face!

Send: $4.25 (check or money order payable to the Treasure Toy House)
Request: #B-148: Heart Sticker
Send to: Treasure Toy House
6010 Lone Oak Rd.
P.O. Box 58
Rockford, MN 55373

National Pastime

Baseball cards have many potential uses in the classroom. Spark an interest in reading with the whole-language approach, illustrate the value of math skills in everyday life, or offer them as a unique reward for work well done. This grab bag is filled with at least 50 cards, all collectibles with advertised values of $5 to $10! Connect history, social studies, sports, mathematics, reading, and more, through a subject students love.

Send: $4.95 (check or money order payable to the Jamestown Stamp Company)
Request: Baseball Card Grab Bag
Send to: Jamestown Stamp Company
        341 East Third St.
        Jamestown, NY 14701-0019

Neatness Counts!

Encourage your students to produce neat and tidy papers by supplying them with the tools to clean up their mistakes! These colorful erasers are about 1″ across and are useful as incentive items, rewards, or a great way to break the ice on that first day of class. This introductory packet contains 100 pieces in assorted colors and designs such as a schoolbus, #1, A+, or Great!

Send: $4.25 (check or money order payable to the Treasure Toy House)
Request: B-149: School Round Eraser
Send to: Treasure Toy House
        6010 Lone Oak Rd.
        P.O. Box 58
        Rockford, MN 55373

Birthday Slide

Every kid loves to feel remembered on his or her special day. It's easy to extend to each of your students that little gesture of personal attention with these colorful birthday puzzles. The 15-piece slide puzzles challenge students' manual dexterity, deductive skills, and spatial awareness, but kids will think it's just fun. This introductory pack contains one dozen puzzles in various designs, all with a "Happy Birthday" message.

Send: $3.80 (check or money order payable to the Treasure Toy House)
Request: #B-185: Birthday Slide Puzzle
Send to: Treasure Toy House
        6010 Lone Oak Rd.
        P.O. Box 58
        Rockford, MN 55373

Magic Screen

Here's a double-duty item that not only lets you convey a personal expression of best wishes on a child's special day, it's also a great way for kids to practice their writing anywhere, anytime! The familiar magic screen can be written on endlessly and wiped clean in a flash. This introductory packet contains a dozen 7″ magic screens, various colorful designs, all with a "Happy Birthday" message.

Send: $3.80 (check or money order payable to the Treasure Toy House)
Request: #B-186: Birthday Magic Screen 7″
Send to: Treasure Toy House
        6010 Lone Oak Rd.
        P.O. Box 58
        Rockford, MN 55373

Space Stuff

Looking for a source of crowd-pleasing science materials and motivational items? CORE offers full-color cut-out space shuttle models that really fly ($3 for eight models), the ever-popular Astronaut Ice Cream ($1.75 per package), authentic space shuttle erasers ($.60 each), NASA logo pencils ($.25 each), and lots more inexpensive space shuttle visual aids. The 100-page catalog also features a wealth of other educational materials.

Send: Your name and address on school stationery
Request: The latest CORE catalog of educational materials
Send to: NASA CORE/Lorain County JVS
      15181 Route 58 South
      Oberlin, OH 44074

For Teachers Only

There's no more basic or necessary tool for teachers and students than pens and pencils. This 56-page full-color catalog contains every kind of writing utensil you could want, all specially discount-priced for educators. Hundreds of choices for pencils sporting facts and figures, ideas to motivate, birthday greetings, or kudos for a job well done. Also dozens of inexpensive puzzles, erasers, stickers, and related reward items.

Send: Your name and address
Request: The latest *For Teachers Only* catalog
Send to: Atlas Pen & Pencil
      3040 North 29th Ave.
      Hollywood, FL 33022

Kids do lots of things that deserve special praise. Bolster your students' self-esteem, reward a project well done, or just let children know how you feel about them with these star stickers. This introductory package contains 100 stickers that sport an assortment of sayings such as Excellent, U-R Special, Good Job, and Great Work! Stickers come in purple, red, and yellow.

Send: $4.25 (check or money order payable to the Treasure Toy House)
Request: #B-150: Star School Stickers
Send to: Treasure Toy House
6010 Lone Oak Rd.
P.O. Box 58
Rockford, MN 55373